ROUTLEDGE LIBRARY EDITIONS:
THE LABOUR MOVEMENT

Volume 9

THE BRITISH CO-OPERATIVE MOVEMENT IN A SOCIALIST SOCIETY

THE BRITISH CO-OPERATIVE MOVEMENT IN A SOCIALIST SOCIETY

G. D. H. COLE

Routledge
Taylor & Francis Group
LONDON AND NEW YORK

First published in 1951 by George Allen & Unwin Ltd

This edition first published in 2019
by Routledge
2 Park Square, Milton Park, Abingdon, Oxon OX14 4RN

and by Routledge
711 Third Avenue, New York, NY 10017

Routledge is an imprint of the Taylor & Francis Group, an informa business

British Library Cataloguing in Publication Data
A catalogue record for this book is available from the British Library

ISBN: 978-1-138-32435-0 (Set)
ISBN: 978-0-429-43443-3 (Set) (ebk)
ISBN: 978-1-138-33638-4 (Volume 9) (hbk)
ISBN: 978-0-429-44303-9 (Volume 9) (ebk)

Publisher's Note
The publisher has gone to great lengths to ensure the quality of this reprint but points out that some imperfections in the original copies may be apparent.

Disclaimer
The publisher has made every effort to trace copyright holders and would welcome correspondence from those they have been unable to trace.

THE COMPOSITION OF CO-OPERATIVE RETAIL TRADE 1948

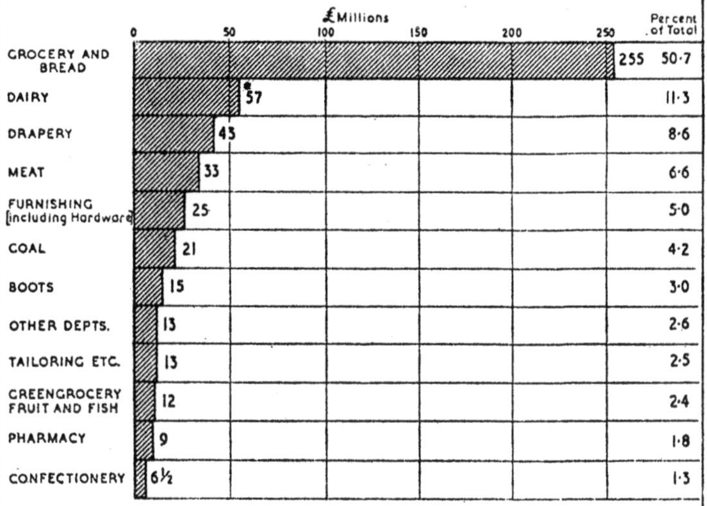

THE CO-OPERATIVE SHARE IN TOTAL RETAIL TRADE 1948

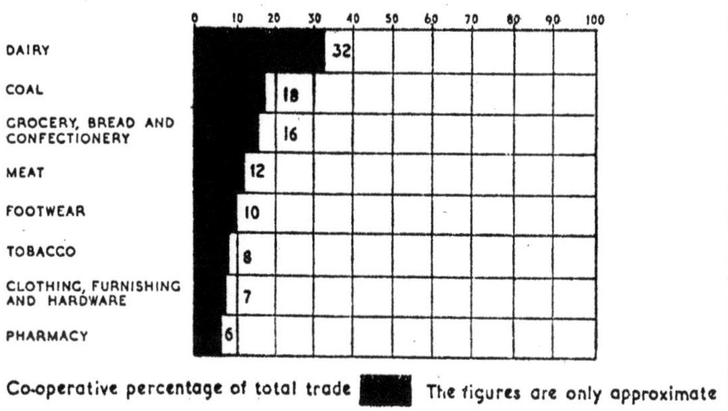

THE BRITISH CO-OPERATIVE MOVEMENT IN A SOCIALIST SOCIETY

by G. D. H. Cole

*

A Report written for the Fabian Society

London

GEORGE ALLEN & UNWIN LTD

RUSKIN HOUSE MUSEUM STREET

FIRST PUBLISHED IN 1951

PRINTED IN GREAT BRITAIN
in 12-point Fournier type
BY HAZELL WATSON & VINEY LTD
AYLESBURY & LONDON

Preface

*

THIS book has been written at the request of the Fabian Society, which was in turn responding to the desire of the Sara Hall Trust for research work bearing on the position and prospects of the British Co-operative movement. It is a personal report by me to these bodies, and in no way commits either of them. Indeed, I expect it to provoke much dissent and to find few to agree with most of its conclusions. The great majority of leading Co-operators will almost certainly dislike it, because they will find the idea of a great competing 'mutual trading' movement under State sponsorship distasteful as well as novel. Nor will most of them like any better the high importance which I attach to the development of Producers' Co-operation—a form of organisation they are apt to treat rather as a rival than as an integral part of the Co-operative movement.

For this reason I wish to make it plain that the Co-operators and Co-operative agencies which have kindly helped me in my work have done so with no knowledge of the conclusions I should draw from my study of the facts. I am particularly grateful to Mr. J. A. Hough, Research Officer of the Co-operative Union, who, in this case as always, has responded most fully to my requests for information. In addition to what I have got from him directly, most of the data given in the Tables come either from the annual volume of *Co-operative Statistics* which he edits or from his admirable series of Research Articles in the *Co-operative Review*. I have also to thank the English and Scottish Co-operative Wholesale Societies, the Co-operative Productive Federation, and the Agricultural Co-operative Association for supplying me with a number of facts and figures, and Dr. N. Barou for reading through my typescript and making a large number of most valuable suggestions. Many of these I accepted gladly: where I held to my own opinion in face of his criticism—as in the case of my proposal to set up a chain of 'Mutual' Societies side by side with the existing Co-operatives—his comments helped me to put my projects into better shape.

In offering this book to my colleagues in the Fabian Society, I wish to stress that I regard it as no more than the beginning of a discussion that ought to have been started a long time ago. If my suggestions are wrong—as I am aware some of them may be —I hope some other Fabian will try his hand at making a better plan. Somebody must do some hard thinking about the relations between Socialism and Co-operation if both movements are not to be stultified. I have 'chanced my arm': now it is someone else's turn.

G. D. H. Cole.

Oxford,
January, 1951

Contents

*

Tables

*

TABLES

Chapter I

BRITISH CO-OPERATION AND ITS LEADERS

*

THE Co-operative movement of Great Britain has more than ten million members, who represent a substantially greater number of individual consumers. The Co-operative Store is a familiar feature in almost every town and in a considerable number of villages over the whole country, and the Co-operative delivery van is met with very frequently in the streets. There are Co-operative factories in many places; Co-operative flour-mills at the big ports; Co-operative centres in many places for the collection and processing of food. There are farmers' Co-operatives, both for the purchasing of agricultural requirements and for the marketing of produce; there are even a few Co-operative farms. Co-operative Insurance offices, Building Society offices and banking establishments do not show up prominently, but they are there. Dozens of Co-operative meetings are being held up and down the country every day—Quarterly Meetings and committee meetings of members of local, federal or wholesale Co-operative Societies, meetings of Co-operative Guilds or young people's organisations, adult classes for Co-operative members and employees, technical classes for apprentices, salesmen and other workers, political meetings of Co-operative Party groups, conferences, week-end schools and simple jollifications. There is a Co-operative College, to which come students of the movement from many countries. There are Co-operative sporting events, organised through special Leagues of Co-operative clubs—football matches, athletic contests and so on. There is much Co-operative music-making and a fair amount of Co-operative play-acting. And there are international as well as national reunions, from summer camps to meetings of the International Co-operative Women's Guild and the International Co-operative

Alliance—the only sections of the 'International' which still include the countries on both sides of the 'iron curtain'.

British Co-operation is, indeed, a very big affair, with which at least one-third of the adult population is connected in one way or another. At its basis lie the thousand or so local retail Co-operative Societies of consumers, of immensely varying size, from village and small-town single shops to vast concerns with many branches and departments and members counted by the hundred thousand. There are a good many other kinds of Co-operative Society besides these; but the local Consumers' Societies account for the great bulk of the membership and of the business activity. In this respect, British Co-operation is unlike the movements in many other countries, in which Agricultural Co-operative Societies are as important as Consumers' Societies, and Co-operative Credit Societies also play a large part. Great Britain has its Agricultural Societies, its Producers' Societies carrying on their own factory production, and a number of other types of Co-operative activity. But here the Consumers' Societies hold so predominant a position that they are often spoken of as if they constituted the entire Co-operative movement—and, indeed, are apt to think of themselves as doing so.

The purpose of the present enquiry is to consider the prospects of the British Co-operative movement in all its main aspects and not as a consumers' movement only. But inevitably, in such a consideration, the Consumers' Societies must loom much larger than the rest. We shall be concerned not so much with the immediate prospects of the development of Co-operative trade and production—a subject on which I have written elsewhere[1]—as with certain problems of the longer run. I am writing on the assumption that the tendency, strongly manifested since 1945, toward an extension of public enterprise and public control over economic developments will continue, though not necessarily in the forms which it has taken so far. On this assumption, I am setting out to enquire how Co-operative enterprise, in its various

[1] In the final section of my centenary history, *A Century of Co-operation* (1945), and in a booklet, *Next Steps in Co-operative Advance*, published by the Co-operative Press (1946).

forms, can best be fitted into the economic structure of the coming society, say, over as much as a generation ahead. I am agreeing with the claim of the Co-operative leaders, put forward in their manifesto on the matter issued early in 1950,[1] that Co-operation is entitled to be regarded as a form of enterprise broadly in compliance with the requirements of a society planned for welfare and accepting the principle of 'fair shares' as the foundation of its economic policies; and I am trying to see over what part of the field that may come to be transferred from 'private enterprise' to some sort of collective system the Co-operative movement, or some adaptation of the Co-operative principle, may provide the best way of satisfying the need for responsibility to the people without more centralisation, bureaucracy and concentration of power than the circumstances of modern society render unavoidable.

I am, in fact, in search of diversity, rather than of uniformity, in the basic structure of the new economic order towards which we are moving at a rapid pace. I am convinced of the need for new forms of economic structure to replace capitalism over a wide field; but, in common with many people, I am somewhat appalled at the prospect of an indefinite multiplication of the but half-responsible National Boards and Commissions to which the administration of the nationalised industries and services has been handed over. I do not like the look of these huge monopolistic organisations, under small groups of men appointed from above by Ministers who can, in the nature of things, exercise over them only a most imperfect control, and answer for their doings only within very narrow limits either to Parliament or to public opinion. I am not saying that the setting-up of these Public Corporations was a mistake; in the circumstances, it may have been, for the industries so far nationalised, the least objectionable short-run solution. But I am sure I do not want to see a great many more of them, and that the method of nationalisation by establishing this sort of industry-wide monopoly cannot with good results be extended over any large further section of the industrial system.

[1] *The Co-operative Movement in a Collectivist Economy.*

Accordingly, as I am even more reluctant to contemplate an indefinite continuance of capitalist enterprise, with all that it involves in the way of wide economic inequality, class-division and the return of unemployment as a weapon for disciplining the workers, I am very eager to explore the possibilities of alternative forms of economic organisation that can be made to satisfy the essential democratic conditions. Among these alternatives, I am eager to explore to the full the potentialities of Co-operation, not only in its existing forms, but also in others which it may be feasible to devise. I therefore approach this enquiry asking rather how great than how small a place can be assigned to Co-operation in the society of the future, and with every wish to enlist the support of the Co-operative leaders for bold developments of Co-operative action—but at the same time with a determination not to allow the conservatism of some of these leaders in clinging to what they already have to be a good ground for obstructing the growth of new forms of socially acceptable enterprise.

This small book, then, is an attempt to assess the importance and the function of the Co-operative method in the coming social order in Great Britain; and it is written in the hope that a clearer vision of the long-run prospects of British Co-operation may be of help in facing the wider economic problems of to-day and to-morrow. As matters stand now, there is an evident danger that the Labour and Co-operative Parties, closely though they are allied, may fall out seriously as soon as the Labour Party is in a position to formulate its plans for the next big advance towards that 'Socialism' which is its professed objective. Even the very modest projects of further nationalisation with which the Labour Party went into the General Election of 1950 evoked from the leaders of the Co-operative movement a doubtful and critical response, most articulate in relation to the proposed taking over of Industrial Insurance, but by no means confined to that one proposal. In that particular matter, the Labour Party Executive promptly beat a retreat, substituting a plan of 'mutualisation' for the original proposal to nationalise. But the fears of the Co-operative leaders were by no means entirely removed: they continued to ask both themselves and the Labour Party Executive what branch of their business might be threatened next, even when the Co-operative Insurance Society had been reprieved. They were worried about the wholesale trade in foodstuffs, which provides a large part of the business of the Co-operative Wholesale Societies; and a casual remark by Lord Shepherd, a former high official of the Labour Party, appearing to threaten a possible incursion of the State into the field of retail trade, set them all a-twitter, even though it was in no sense a pronouncement made on the Labour Party's behalf.

The plain truth is that, though the Labour and Co-operative Parties have been working together both in Parliament and in the constituencies for more than thirty years, there has never been any real attempt to reach any comprehensive agreement between them on long-run objectives. Hitherto, their immediate objectives have been nearly enough the same for no important causes of division to arise beyond occasional quarrels over constituency organisation and allocation of seats for Co-operative Party candidates. The representatives of the Co-operative movement have worked in harmony with those of the Labour Party and the Trades Union Congress on the National Council of Labour since the Co-operators joined that body in 1941. But neither on the N.C.L. nor elsewhere has long-run policy come up for serious discussion until quite lately—in fact, not until the draft Labour Party programme of 1949 brought the matter suddenly to a head.

When this did happen, I think neither the Labour Party nor the Co-operative leaders felt at all satisfied about their respective positions, nor at all confident that they knew what they wanted to say. As long as it was a question of nationalising basic services, such as railways, docks, canals, road passenger transport, gas, electricity and water supply, civil aviation or the Bank of England, no existing Co-operative interests were affected, and the Co-operators, as Co-operators, had little or nothing to say. In coal-mining they had a tiny interest, and a few regrets were heard at the loss of Shilbottle colliery and of certain land that had been bought by the movement with a view to possible mining development. But the need to reorganise the coal-mining industry under some form of unified control was seen to be so overwhelming, and the direct Co-operative interest was so small, that no serious objections were raised. In the case of road haulage there would have been much stronger objection had not the Government accepted the exclusion of the 'C' licence holders—that is, of firms transporting their own goods in their own lorries—but, this conceded, the Co-operators had nothing to worry about. Nor had Co-operators any direct interest in the steel industry.[1] In effect, not one of the nationalisation measures enacted between 1945 and 1950 involved any important Co-operative interest; and Co-operators were in a position to make up their minds about them without having to consider, save in quite a general way, how their movement would be affected by them.

The programme of the Co-operative Party, indeed, had for a long time included advocacy of the nationalisation of the basic industries and services to which the Labour Government applied its measures after 1945. The views of the Co-operative Party do not, however, necessarily reflect in such a matter the attitude of the Co-operative movement as a whole. Although the Party has a nominal affiliated membership of nearly nine millions and has most of the important Co-operative Societies' support, only a small proportion of its nominal adherents take any active part in it, and the final control of Co-operative policy rests, not with the Party, but with the annual Co-operative Congress, which represents all sections of the movement. The Congress gives its blessing to the Party, which certainly could not adopt any programme of which a majority of the Congress delegates would disapprove. But, all the same, there is a difference: the Co-operative Party represents the views, neither of the ten million Co-operative members, nor of the, say, one per cent. of these millions who take some active part in the management of the local Co-operative Societies, but of a distinct, politically interested minority that overlaps extensively with the membership of the local Labour Parties, and leaves out the still considerable body of active Co-operators who regret that their movement ever founded a party and cling to the old tradition of political neutrality

[1] Except as consumers, and only on a very small scale at that.

from which it broke away only in 1917. These sections of the active Co-operative membership include a substantial number of Liberals, and some Conservatives, besides some who refuse to accept any party label. For the most part, they regard Co-operation as good business and, as Co-operators, dislike the rival forms of economic organisation with which they are competitors in the market. But, though they dislike Capitalism and small-scale private enterprise when they come into conflict with them, they tend to regard Co-operation, not as the basis for an alternative social system or as the partner of Socialism in creating such a system, but simply as a convenient way of serving the consumers' interests in certain fields of trade and production; and accordingly they are inclined to take for granted the continuance of capitalism as an environment within which Co-operation can be developed without any comprehensive transformation of the entire economic system. They feel themselves at war, not with capitalism, but only with some of its manifestations—with the private trader and with the monopolistic combines which dominate certain branches of manufacture—if even that. For not a few of them who are active on the trading side of the movement, Co-operation is simply one form of business organisation, in which they have grown up and in the success of which their interests and activities are involved; and they do not look beyond the immediate business concerns of their Societies to any distant future, or seriously consider any notion of Co-operation as the forerunner of a new social order.

It has to be kept constantly in mind that no more than a small minority of the ten million Co-operators take any interest at all in Co-operative affairs, beyond using the Co-operative Store as a convenience for the purchase of some part of their household requirements. The majority of Co-operators buy a large part of their supplies from non-Co-operative agencies; not a few use the Co-operative Store for no more than a few kinds of purchase—say bread, or milk, or coal; and for many more it is mainly the grocery store that pays a dividend on purchases—a convenience to the housewife who wishes to save up in order to meet claims that accrue over longer periods than a week, or to build up a small reserve of purchasing power against an emergency. There is no *necessary* connection between the Co-operative movement and any sort of social idealism; indeed, the movement has grown to so vast a size mainly because there is no such connection. Co-operation has had from the beginning, and has never lost, its idealistic aspects; but it has never limited its appeal to those for whom its ideals count. Nor has it recruited its leadership exclusively among the idealists; even if most of its leaders season their speeches, and their own thinking, with some reference to Co-operative ideals, in action a high proportion of them are merely traders committed to a certain way of trading and somewhat impatient of such colleagues as wish, not merely to talk about the ideals of Co-operation, but to allow their practice to be influenced by them.

The Consumers' Co-operative movement has, indeed, a curiously compartmental structure. It is run, on its business side, by two distinct groups of persons, whose relative authorities are by no means clearly defined. On the one hand there are the 'lay' Committees of Management, which, subject to members' meetings, control, at any rate in theory, the local Consumers' Societies and, through their elected delegates, the Districts, Sections and national Committees of the Co-operative Union, and also the various Federal Societies set up by groups of local Societies for the conduct of particular kinds of enterprise. Side by side with these 'lay' representatives, who keep the committee posts at all levels firmly in their own hands through a widespread system of elections, are the full-time officials who have the day-to-day management of the business of the local and Federal Societies, but are usually excluded from holding any elective office at the higher levels. These officials have their own separate organisations, not only for professional purposes, but also for the co-ordination of their trading activities in national trade associations concerned with particular branches of Co-operative activity—meat, milk, coal, pharmacy and so on. There is a bridge between these two groups in the Wholesale Societies, whose directors, drawn mainly from the 'lay' membership, become full-time servants of the movement, and thus tend to pass into the official group without losing their eligibility to take part in the higher control of policy. But, in general, Co-operative committee-men (and women) and Co-operative officials (nearly all men) constitute two quite separate groups; and there is no such domination of the higher policy-making bodies by full-time officials as exists in the Trade Union movement. Indeed, it is quite the other way round: the trading officials of the Co-operative movement, except the directors of the Wholesale Societies, have practically no recognised share in policy-making, however influential some of them may be in practice in the affairs of the local Societies they serve.

Side by side with this dual trading structure the Co-operative movement has a largely separate educational and propagandist structure, characterised by some of the same features. Most local Societies of any substantial size have Educational Committees quite distinct from their Management Committees, and separately elected. Often election to the Educational Committee is a stepping-stone to a seat on the Management Committee; but there are many committee members who confine their activities to the educational side. Here, too, the regional and national structure of the movement is built up on a foundation of 'lay' control; and the educational officials form a separate group, excluded from election to the higher committees. But in this field there is a third group, overlapping with the lay membership of the Educational (and also to some extent of the Management) Committees. This is made up of what are called, in Co-operative parlance, the 'Auxiliary Bodies', by far the most important element being the Co-operative Women's Guilds. The relatively weak British Federation of Young Co-operators also belongs in this class. The Guilds are attached locally to the local Consumers' Societies, but have also their own parallel regional and national organisation, based on the all-pervasive principle of 'lay' control. Finally, the Co-operative Party has its own separate structure, local and national, based on a curious mixture of lay-controlled Local Parties and Political Councils and of 'Society members'—that is, of local Consumers' Societies, which are directly affiliated to the national Co-operative Party.

The system of 'lay' control which dominates Co-operative

organisation is in form highly democratic; but, in face of the apathy of most Co-operative members and of the usually small attendance at local members' meetings, it has produced the result of the emergence of a class of 'professional laymen', who, while earning their livings mostly outside the Co-operative movement, make service on Co-operative committees a regular by-employment, for which small—usually very small—payments are received. These regular committee-men form a distinctly recognisable element in the Co-operative membership, serving, not only on the committees of their local Societies, but also on those of the host of regional, federal and specialist organisations which the movement has thrown off—District and Sectional Committees of the Co-operative Union, Federal Societies for dairying, laundries, coal distribution and many other purposes, right up to the national committees of the Co-operative Union. Delegates to the Co-operative Congress, which is the final policy-making authority, as far as there is one—for the Congress has no power to bind the independent local Societies—are drawn mainly from this group, which forms the 'conscious minority' among the ten million individual members. On this body of some thousands of active 'laymen' Co-operative democracy really rests. But it is a democracy qualified by the failure of more than a small minority of the membership to play any part even in electing its representatives. It should be added that the elections to regional and federal bodies are made mostly by the Committees of the local Societies, and not by the general body of members: so that the local 'lay' Committees are the dominant factor in determining the composition of the higher leadership.

This structure was never deliberately planned: for the most part it simply grew up as the movement expanded from its original foundation in the local Consumers' Societies. At first, these were controlled by their 'lay' Committees, for the simple reason that there was no one else to do the job—for at the outset there were few, and in many cases no, full-time managers. While membership remained relatively small, a high proportion of members took an active part in Quarterly Meetings and in elections, so that the elected Committees were under substantial control by the bulk of the membership. Then, as the movement grew, the proportion of active members fell sharply and the effective powers of the elected Committees increased; and at the same time the numbers and importance of the full-time officials grew rapidly. The basis of 'lay', as against official, control had, however, by this time become firmly established; and it has been maintained ever since. Most of the active members of the local Societies regard it as the very foundation of Co-operative 'democracy', and remain jealous of any proposal to allow the full-time officials a share in representation on the higher policy-making bodies. There is almost as sharp a division between 'lay' representatives and officials as there is between Members of Parliament and Civil Servants or between municipal Councillors and local government officers.

The effect of this system is to give the Co-operative leadership, for both good and ill, a certain parochial quality.

TABLE I

RETAIL CONSUMERS' CO-OPERATIVE SOCIETIES. NUMBERS, MEMBERSHIP AND SIZE, 1948

Section	*No. of Societies*	*No. of Members* 000*s*	*Societies with more than*		*Societies with less than*	
			95,000	50,000*	1,000†	500
Irish	17	113	Belfast	1	12	8
Midland	124	1,552	Birmingham	8	39	23
Northern	102	818	—	2	19	9
North-eastern	145	1,182	Barnsley, Leeds	5	48	23
North-western	199	1,807	Liverpool, Manchester	7	66	41
Scottish	205	1,180	Edinburgh	3	36	16
Southern	106	2,744	London, Royal Arsenal, South Suburban	6	7	5
South-western	71	448	—	2	15	8
Western	61	319	—	—	17	5
TOTAL .	1,030	10,162	10	34	259	138

* Including those with more than 95,000.

† Including those with fewer than 500.

TABLE II

RETAIL CO-OPERATIVE SOCIETIES. SIZES (BY SECTIONS), 1948

Sections	*Irish*	*Scottish*	*Northern*	*North-eastern*	*North-western*	*Midland*	*Southern*	*South-western*	*Western*	*Totals*	*Per cent. of Total*
Under 500	9	17	9	24	41	23	5	8	6	142	14·0
500–1,000	3	19	10	25	24	16	2	7	11	117	11·0
1,000–2,000	2	44	15	33	25	16	11	20	19	185	18·0
2,000–5,000	1	65	29	25	37	19	25	20	13	234	22·0
5,000–10,000	1	30	20	14	27	16	26	7	14	155	15·0
10,000–20,000	—	16	9	12	19	14	16	4	6	96	9·0
20,000–35,000	—	12	6	4	14	10	7	3	1	57	5·0
35,000–50,000	—	—	2	4	4	1	7	—	1	19	2·0
50,000–75,000	—	2	1	2	4	5	4	—	—	18	2·0
75,000–100,000	1	—	1	1	1	3	—	2	—	9	1·0
100,000–200,000	—	—	—	2	2	—	—	—	—	4	0·4
200,000–300,000	—	—	—	—	—	1	1	—	—	2	0·2
300,000–500,000	—	—	—	—	—	—	1	—	—	1	0·1
Over 500,000	—	—	—	—	—	—	1	—	—	1	0·1
TOTALS	17	205	102	146	198	124	106	71	71	1,040	100

One-quarter of all Societies have fewer than 1,000 members.
Nearly two-thirds of all Societies have fewer than 5,000 members.
Four-fifths of all Societies have fewer than 10,000 members.

TABLE III

THE LARGEST RETAIL CO-OPERATIVE SOCIETIES, 1948

			Membership thousands
	1.	London*	937
1 million	2.	Royal Arsenal	338
	3.	Birmingham	270
	4.	South Suburban	224
	5.	Liverpool	180
2 millions	6.	Leeds	141
	7.	Barnsley	112
	8.	Manchester and Salford	110
	9.	Belfast	99
	10.	Bristol	95
	11.	Derby	94
	12.	Plymouth	90
	13.	Brightside	90
	14.	Nottingham	89
	15.	St. Cuthbert's (Edinburgh)	88
3 millions	16.	Birkenhead	86
	17.	Newcastle-on-Tyne	85
	18.	Leicester	77
	19.	Walsall	75
	20.	Portsea Island	73
	21.	Sheffield	71
	22.	Burslem	70
	23.	Brighton	68
	24.	Aberdeen, North	66
	25.	Coventry	65
	26.	Hull	62
	27.	Peterborough	62
	28.	Grays	60
	29.	Glasgow, Kinning Park	59
4 millions	30.	Ten Acres and Stirchley	58
	31.	Bolton	57
	32.	Preston	56
	33.	Middlesbrough	55
	34.	Enfield Highway	55
	35.	Blackpool	54
	36.	Mansfield Woodhouse	53
	37.	Ipswich	50
	38.	Reading	48
	39.	Stockton	47
	40.	Oxford	46
	41.	Watford	45
	42.	Darlington	43
	43.	Luton	42
	44.	Doncaster	42
	45.	Huddersfield	42
	46.	Eccles	41
	47.	Gloucester	40
	48.	Bradford	40
	49.	Colchester	40
	50.	Rotherham	39
	51.	Warrington	38
5 millions	52.	Lancaster	36
	53.	Beswick (Manchester)	36
	54.	Cambridge	36
	55.	Lincoln	35

* Now (1951) more than one million.

TABLE IV

Co-operative Membership and Trade per Head: Distribution by Counties, 1948

Membership as Percentage of Total Population

39. Northamptonshire
30. Durham, Northumberland, Nottinghamshire
29. Derbyshire
28. Worcestershire
27. Cumberland
26. Lancashire
25. Yorkshire, Leicestershire
24. Oxfordshire
23. Warwickshire, Greater London*
22. Cheshire, Devonshire, Denbighshire
21. Suffolk, Bedfordshire
20. Westmorland
18. Staffordshire, Cambridgeshire, Dorset, Wiltshire
17. Buckinghamshire, Somerset, Gloucestershire
16. Lincolnshire
15. Glamorgan
14. Hertfordshire, Cornwall, Montgomeryshire
12. Norfolk, Hampshire, Berkshire, Monmouthshire, Flintshire
11. Shropshire
10. Kent
9. Sussex, Carmarthenshire, Caernarvonshire
7. Essex,† Merionethshire
6. Pembrokeshire
5. Herefordshire
4. Cardiganshire, Anglesey
3. Huntingdonshire, Breconshire
0. Rutland,‡ Radnor‡

Sales per Head

£	
19	Northumberland, Northamptonshire
17	Durham, Nottinghamshire
15	Cumberland, Derbyshire
13	Worcestershire, Oxon
12	Yorkshire, Lancashire, Cheshire, Leicestershire
10	Warwickshire, Suffolk, Gloucestershire, Glamorgan
9	Bedfordshire, Devonshire
8	Westmorland, Staffordshire, Lincolnshire, Greater London,* Buckinghamshire, Cambridgeshire, Denbighshire
7	Wiltshire, Somerset, Monmouthshire
6	Kent, Hampshire, Dorset, Cornwall, Carmarthenshire
5	Shropshire, Norfolk, Berkshire, Hertfordshire, Montgomeryshire, Flintshire
4	Caernarvonshire
3	Essex,† Sussex, Merionethshire
2	Hampshire, Pembrokeshire, Cardiganshire, Anglesey
1	Huntingdonshire, Breconshire
0	Rutland,‡ Radnor‡

* London County, Middlesex and Surrey.

† The figures for Essex are misleading, as the suburban areas are served by the London Societies.

‡ There are no Societies with headquarters in these counties.

Note.—The entire membership of each Society is assigned to the county in which its headquarters are situated.

Chapter II

THE IDEALS OF CO-OPERATION

*

THE men of Rochdale, when they set up their Pioneers' Co-operative Society more than a century ago, began in a small way with a small grocery store in T'Owd Lane. But already they had great ambitions, which they set down in their statement of their objects:

> "That, as soon as practicable, this Society shall proceed to arrange the powers of production, distribution, education and government; or, in other words, to establish a self-supporting home colony of united interests, or assist other societies in establishing such colonies."

The phrasing of this object was Owenite: the men who wrote it were Owenite Socialists, followers of Robert Owen and believers in a new social system which they thought would speedily replace capitalism and bring with it an epoch of assured happiness for the human race. The word 'Socialist' in those days meant 'Owenite', and had hardly, in Great Britain, any other meaning. The preceding organisation out of which the Pioneers' Society grew had been called the Socialist Institution, and had been a branch of the Owenite movement. The name 'home colony of united interests' was in regular use among the Owenite Socialists, for what Owen had called, earlier on, 'Villages of Co-operation', —local communities in which men, women and children would live, produce, consume and gain the benefits of education in common, and would govern their own affairs so as to have little to do with the governments of the 'old, immoral world'. Indeed, they hoped before long to render such governments obsolete and unnecessary, as all the peoples, recognising the advantages of the Socialist, or Co-operative, system, set up their own communities and did away with the need for any government save their own local self-government, supplemented by loose, co-operative relationships between the several home colonies of the New Moral World.

In 1844 in Great Britain, Socialism and Co-operation meant, not two different things, but a single gospel. It had never occurred to the Owenite Socialists that Socialism meant, or even involved, 'nationalisation' or the taking over of the ownership and conduct of industry by the State. The form of common ownership to which they looked forward was essentially local: the Home Colonies were to be owned by those who lived in them, and their members were to produce in common what was needed for their own consumption or for exchange with other Colonies in order to procure such goods as they did not make for themselves. Not merely Great Britain, but the whole world, the Owenites believed, would be transformed quite soon into a Co-operative Commonwealth made up of local communities, each resting on the principle of mutual service and educating the new generations in the spirit of Socialist fellowship.

The aims of these Co-operative pioneers were not limited to Co-operative store-keeping; nor did this occupy a large place in their thoughts of the future. They began with a grocery shop, because, after trying and failing with a Co-operative Weaving Society, the shop seemed to them the most hopeful way of making a start. They meant to go on from this beginning to a number of further projects, short of their long-run objective of establishing 'a self-supporting home colony'. They meant to build, or buy, a group of houses in which 'those members desiring to assist one another in improving their domestic and social condition' could live together as neighbours; they meant to begin manufacturing, with their own members as their employees; they announced their intention of purchasing or renting and of cultivating with their members' labour 'an estate or estates of land'. In short, they intended to feel their way by stages from mere shopkeeping on a mutual basis to the achievement of their comprehensive Co-operative Socialist ideal. In their eyes competitive capitalism was the enemy to be fought with all the weapons at their command; and the purpose was to replace capitalism, with its setting of man against man and its reliance on profit as the driving force of production, by a new way of life resting on free, mutual service.

These Owenite Socialist objectives dropped speedily into the background as the Rochdale Pioneers achieved and settled down to solid business success within a more limited field. They did take some action towards several of their intermediate objectives. They did build a number of houses for their members—but not as a compact settlement such as they had thought of at the outset or with any special measures for improving the domestic and social condition of those who lived in them. They did found both a Manufacturing Society for textiles and a Corn Mill, but in such ways that the Manufacturing Society drifted out of connection with the Pioneers' Society, and the Corn Mill became in effect a federal concern, mainly owed by a group of Consumers' Societies which bought its output. These various ventures, instead of serving as half-way houses towards the complete Villages of Co-operation which had been thought of at the outset, drifted into independence; and the Pioneers' thoughts turned instead to the creation of a Wholesale Society, to be owned and controlled jointly by their own Consumers' Society and by as many others as they could induce to take part with them.

The Wholesale Society was duly established, and achieved before long a remarkable success. Quite early in its advance, it branched out into production, setting up its own factories for the making of certain goods for which there was an assured demand in the local distributive Stores. It reached out overseas, setting up its foreign depôts for the purchase of a wide range of supplies —mainly foodstuffs. It gradually built up a fleet of vessels to transport its goods; it took up banking and insurance and a number of other activities that developed naturally out of its relations with the local Societies, which were its joint owners and beneficiaries. At first there was a good deal of doubt concerning the right way of conducting these far-flung federal Co-operative ventures; and many of the older Co-operators were unhappy at the fact that their movement was becoming a large-scale employer of workers who, as workers, were given no share in the control of the establishments in which they worked. These older men saw Co-operation as a movement, not of consumers only, but of producers and consumers—who were, of course, largely the same persons—in active partnership; they did not like the idea of the consumers employing the producers on terms not very different from those of capitalist employment. They attempted to meet part of the problem by means of profit-sharing in the Wholesale and Retail Societies, and another part by urging the Consumers' Societies, including the Wholesales, to trade actively with the Producers' Societies, where they existed, and to help in creating new ones.

These views, however, failed to appeal to the new generation of Co-operators, who had entered the movement in great numbers as its business success became apparent, and had been attracted in many cases by its value as an agency for the secure investment of small savings on favourable terms. These newcomers were uninfluenced by the old Owenite and Christian Socialist idealism, and regarded the Co-operative movement exclusively as a consumers' organisation for the supply of unadulterated goods at fair prices, reduced in fact by the payment of dividends on purchases, and for the safe investment of savings. Most of them had no use for Co-operative idealism, and less than none for any sort of Socialism; but they were reinforced by a few, including one outstanding leader, John Mitchell, who brought into the movement an essentially different ideal, and one that had great strength because, in the name of idealism, it offered just what the non-idealists wanted. Mitchell, out of strong personal conviction, made exclusive consumers' control into an ideal, and fought for it hard against Owenites and Christian Socialists, who held to the old basis of partnership between producers and consumers in the control of the movement. Mitchell made a philosophy of consumers' control, and in its name declared war on all ideas of co-partnership of the employees in the control of Co-operative production as well as of Co-operative wholesale and retail trade. He was victorious all along the line: under his leadership British Co-operation became consciously the predominantly consumers' movement it has remained ever since.

In this there was great loss, as well as great commercial gain. Undoubtedly, under Mitchell's single-minded leadership and forceful pursuit of his ideals, both Wholesale and Retail Co-operation went ahead with remarkable business success. But Mitchell's ideal, though it was for him and for a few others a real ideal, had little power to impose itself as an ideal on the main body of Co-operators, precisely because it did not require them to do anything at all that they could not have been led to do by entirely selfish motives. Indeed, it even encouraged them to do things that were positively bad, by serving as a justification to Management Committees to conduct their Societies' affairs as if there were no interests other than the consumers' to be taken into account. To-day, the Co-operative movement ranks as a good employer; but in Mitchell's days there were no Trade Unions at all in the distributive trades and very few Trade Unionists in the trades in which the Wholesale Societies developed most of their production. No doubt Co-operative wages and conditions were at any rate as good as those conceded by most of the movement's competitors; but that is not saying much, and there was hardly any notion among the main body of Co-operators, or even of the Co-operative Management Committees and officials, that the movement's employees were entitled to any special consideration—much less to any place in the control of its affairs.

I have put this point strongly—and I know that many Co-operators will consider that I am being unjust. Of course there were always exceptions to what I have been saying; and of course matters have improved a great deal to-day, not only because of the growth of Trade Unions and of the Co-operative-Labour alliance, but also because the attitude of active Co-operators has changed. I am not accusing present-day Co-operators of paying no attention to their employees' well-being. But I am pointing out that the Consumers' Co-operative movement grew up in hard and unsympathetic times, that its business success necessarily attracted a great body of members who did not care a rush for its social ideals, and that the nature of the Mitchell philosophy of Co-operation was such as to make it difficult to bring the bulk of the membership to any attitude of valuing Co-operation except for what they could get out of it.

It is, no doubt, a part answer to argue that the Co-operatives, being in very keen competition with the various forms of private and capitalist trade, could not afford to do anything that might have handicapped them in their business. But to accept this as a sufficient answer would mean throwing a great deal of the case for Co-operation out of the window. It must surely be accepted as a necessary part of the aims of Co-operation, even in its most rigidly exclusive form of consumers' control, to benefit the consumers legitimately and fairly, and not at the employees' expense. The consumer has no better right than the capitalist to exploit the producer; and where consumers behave pretty much like capitalist employers, they cannot expect to be regarded in a very different light. In respect of wages and conditions of work, the Co-operative Societies rank to-day as good employers, but not as outstandingly different from the better of their rivals. In respect of wages they cannot, in face of the great levelling-up that has come about in recent years, afford to be very different from the general run of employers. But conditions are another matter—at any rate, human conditions as distinct from those which are closely bound up with the weekly wage. What worries me is that the Consumers' Co-operatives, while improving their material standards of employment, have done so little to bring back the old spirit of partnership between consumers and producers which originally inspired the movement. In spirit, the main body of the consumers' movement is still dominated by the feeling of exclusive consumers' right, which took hold of it during the hard times of Victorianism and has never since let go.

What am I asking, by way of change? Mainly two things. In the first place, I want to see a much greater willingness to encourage the growth of *producers'*, as well as of consumers', Co-operation—to put capital into Producers' Societies and to buy their goods, and to give the Co-operative Productive Federation a much bigger place in the counsels of the movement. Secondly, I want to see the whole question of the *status* of the Co-operative employees—retail, wholesale trading and productive—taken up again, with the purpose of finding a solution that will give them a real participation in the movement's affairs and a real sense of sharing in the control of the work on which they are engaged.

On this second point, I should like to make as clear as I can what I do *not* mean. I do not at all favour the system that allows Co-operative employees to stand for election to the Management Committees of the Societies which employ them in competition with other members. Such a system is apt to encourage either cabals by the employees to capture control of the Committees, or counter-cabals to keep them out. If the employees are to be represented on Management Committees, as I personally believe they should be, right up to the C.W.S. itself, the appropriate method is to assign certain seats to them and to disallow their standing for others. This is best, because it makes the chosen employees the representatives explicitly of their fellow-workers, instead of tempting them to sail under false colours as the chosen of the general membership. Moreover, this form of representation carries with it a definite recognition of right, and thus re-establishes the old principle of partnership. In practice, employee members of a Management Committee are much less liable to form a dangerous pressure group when their position is explicitly recognised than when it is not.

Co-operators, however, often object to *any* form of employee representation on the ground that it is the consumers' money that is at stake, and that the employees have no further claim beyond being paid fairly for their services and given reasonable security of employment. If the Consumers' Co-operative movement were merely a kind of trading business, similar in most respects to other kinds, and were content to be so regarded, this objection would be valid; but, whatever may be the attitude of a large number of the members, this is not the light in which the active leaders and members wish it to be looked on. The latter, at any rate, do make idealistic claims; and even when such claims are made on behalf of the consumers, and the rights of the consumers are most strongly asserted, it must not be overlooked that rights carry obligations with them—not least the obligation to get on decent human terms with those whom the consumers employ.

I do not suggest anything that would either take away the consumers' final control, exercised by the Quarterly Meetings of members, or deprive the representatives of the general membership of a handsome majority on the Management Committees—for to alter these things would fundamentally change the character of the Consumers' Societies. But, short of this, an element of minority representation on Management Committees, granted as a human right and as a token of partnership, could, I believe, make a great and salutary difference to the spirit and efficiency of the movement, if it were generally introduced, and if at the same time the employees were given a similar representation on the governing bodies of the Co-operative Union.

On the other matter—that of giving a greater place to the Producers' Societies—I shall have a good deal to say later in this book, and need therefore deal with it only in a few words at this point. Most of the so-called Producers' Societies are already, in practice, examples of producer-consumer partnership and not of exclusive producer control. Their capital is to a substantial extent subscribed by the Consumers' Societies, which also buy most of their products; and their boards or committees include a substantial proportion of consumers' nominees. I regard this as salutary, and have no wish to alter it; for I am no more enamoured of exclusive control by producers than by consumers. What I am asking is that, instead of merely tolerating the Producers' Societies that are already well established, the Co-operative movement as a whole should make a real effort to establish new ones, where suitable opportunities can be found, and should cease to regard any expansion of the Producers' Societies as a regrettable form of rivalry with the Wholesale Societies. These latter, as well as the retail Consumers' Societies, ought to welcome the development of new Producers' Societies as a means of avoiding undue uniformity and of encouraging diversity and emulation within the Co-operative movement. There is already some danger of the business of the C.W.S. becoming unduly large for its present organisation and too miscellaneous to be really well managed from a single centre; and if Co-operators mean seriously their statement—with which I agree—that most kinds of manufacture of consumption goods are better suited to Co-operative organisation than to nationalisation, they will have to begin thinking of new and diversified ways of bringing these types of production under Co-operative auspices. They might well, for example, give some of their Federal Societies, set up jointly by groups of neighbouring Consumers' Societies for particular trades, the wider form of consumer-producer partnerships.

This matter I shall be following up later on. My main contention here is that the Co-operative movement, if it is to make good the large claims it has advanced since it has seen the tide of nationalisation flowing in its direction, will have to think not only in a bigger but also in a less stereotyped way, devising new forms of Co-operative enterprise to meet changing social and political conditions, and at the same time trying to get back some of the idealism which, on its trading side, it has so largely lost. No one who knows the Co-operative movement well can help seeing how loose is the connection between the idealistic teaching of the Co-operative educators and propagandists and the day-to-day business affairs of Co-operative trade and production. Almost the movement's right hand does not know what its left hand is doing; and the separation is aggravated by the fact that the two sides are largely in the hands of different persons. Closer integration between the trading and non-trading sides is imperatively needed if the case for a great development of Co-operative enterprise as a recognised alternative to nationalisation is to be made acceptable; and one important means of putting this case across to the Labour movement is to bring back the producers into that partnership with the consumers that was an essential element in the social philosophy of the Co-operative pioneers.

Chapter III

CO-OPERATIVE TRADE AND PROSPECTS

*

THE British Consumers' Co-operative movement, with its ten million shareholding members and its far-flung organisation of local stores all over the country, is immensely bigger than any single capitalist enterprise, and ramifies, through its productive departments, into a wide range of industries. It has been growing steadily, with hardly a serious interruption, for more than a hundred years: the Rochdale Pioneers, who are looked back to as its founders in its modern form, celebrated their centenary in 1944. The thousand or so Local Co-operative Societies, through their twenty-five thousand or so stores and branch shops, serve about thirteen million registered customers with sugar and butter, and rather smaller numbers with other rationed goods. They hold in all almost one-third of the total retail trade in milk and other dairy produce, about one-sixth of the trade in bread, confectionery and groceries, and about one-eighth of the trade in meat. The food trades have been from the first the primary field of Co-operative enterprise; but outside this field the Societies hold between one-fifth and one-sixth of the trade in coal, one-tenth in boots and shoes, eight per cent. in tobacco and cigarettes, six or seven per cent. in clothing, furnishings and hardware, and about six per cent. in pharmacy, besides smaller proportions in many other kinds of goods and services.

THE STRUCTURE OF CO-OPERATIVE TRADE

The Local Consumers' Societies upon which this immense trading structure rests have a common pattern of democratic organisation, but differ very greatly in size. The largest, the London Co-operative Society, which covers only a part of the London area north of the Thames, has recently reached a million members; at the other extreme are village societies with only a few score and with but a single shop, dealing mainly in groceries. Some Societies—such as Plymouth in the south-west and Barnsley British in Yorkshire—cover very large areas round the towns after which they are named; and for many years there has been a gradual process of absorption of small Societies by their larger neighbours or of fusion of a number of small Societies to create larger areas of service. This process, however, has been slow. The small local Societies, especially in the North of England and in Scotland, are extremely tenacious of their independence, and often federal arrangements, under which neighbouring societies have joined in forming a Federal Society for some particular branch of trade—such as laundrying or baking—have been preferred to outright amalgamations. Right up to 1949, though a few local arrangements had been made for 'inter-trading', in order to allow members of outlying societies to make purchases at the central emporium of the nearest big-town society, each local Co-operative Society was an entirely separate trading unit, and membership of a society in one place conferred no rights of purchasing from other societies' stores. Then at length came the institution of a scheme of 'national membership', accepted by the vast majority of the Societies all over the country. This scheme allows a member of any participating Society to trade at any other's shops, and to receive on his purchases a 'dividend' as if he belonged to the Society from which his purchase is made. National membership, in its existing form, involves very elaborate book-keeping, and during the first year of its working its effects do not seem to have been very great. It has, however, evidently a big potential importance both in checking loss of custom when members migrate from place to place and in bringing more unity into the movement. It is likely to make amalgamations easier and to stimulate the growth of large, centrally situated department stores serving wide areas with kinds of goods that cannot be satisfactorily supplied except on a scale which allows big and diversified stocks to be held.

TABLE V

CO-OPERATIVE RETAIL OUTLETS, 1946

	*Number of Societies with Sales Points**	*Number of Societies with Separate Shops*	*Number of Separate Shops*
Department Stores . . .	—	77	127
(This means Stores with numerous inter-connected departments, distinct from the grouping of a number of separate specialist shops on a single site.)			
Grocery, Provisions, Bread, Confectionery and Cooked Meats	1,027	1,027	11,567
Greengrocery, Fruit, Florist, Fish	812	332	1,217
Dairy	583	—	361
Drapery	968	800	1,972
Tailoring and Outfitting . .	772	375	694
Boot and Shoe . . .	939	519	1,068
Furnishing, Hardware, Jewellery, Radio, Electrical and Cycle .	959	517	1,017
Chemists	331	248	724
Hairdressing	—	119	176
Coal	727	—	—
Miscellaneous	—	—	1,052
including:			
Tobacco	—	—	361
Paints and Wallpaper .	—	—	96
Optical	—	—	49
Travel Bureau . . .	—	—	45
Sweets	—	—	31
Corn and Seed . .	—	—	27
Beer, Wine and Spirits .	—	—	18
Ice-cream . . .	—	—	15
Newspapers and Books .	—	—	11
Chiropody . . .	—	—	9
Fried Fish and Chips .	—	—	6
Sports Outfitting . .	—	—	6
Others	—	—	6

* I.e. regularly selling the kind of goods in question.

TABLE V—*continued*

Co-operative Retail Outlets, 1946

	*Number of Societies with Sales Points**	*Number of Societies with Separate Shops*	*Number of Separate Shops*
Cafés and Restaurants . .	—	170	207
Hotels	—	—	11
Cinemas	—	—	11

* I.e. regularly selling the kind of goods in question.

Note.—In this Table each shop is counted only once, even if it has more than one department; but separate shops on contiguous sites are counted separately. The returns cover practically the whole of the local Consumers' Societies connected with the Co-operative Union.

TABLE VI

Co-operative Trade Figures Adjusted to Changing Prices and Cost of Living

A. Total Retail Sales

£ million	*Actual* (*a*)	*Price Index* (*b*)	*Adjusted by* (*b*) (*c*)	*Official Cost of Living Index* (*d*)	*Adjusted by* (*d*) (*e*)
1938	263·3	100	263·3	156	263·3
1939	272·3	103	264·4	158	268·8
1940	298·9	124	241·0	184	253·4
1941	302·2	140	215·9	199	236·9
1942	319·4	150	213·0	200	249·2
1943	331·6	154	215·3	199	259·9
1944	352·3	157	224·4	201	273·4
1945	361·1	161	224·3	203	277·5
1946	402·5	165	243·9	203½	308·5
1947	443·7	185	239·8	205*	337·7

* Estimated for July–December.

TABLE VI—*continued*

CO-OPERATIVE TRADE FIGURES ADJUSTED TO CHANGING PRICES AND COST OF LIVING

B. Sales per Member

£ million	*Actual* (*a*)	*Adjusted by Price Index* (*b*)	*Adjusted by Cost-of-living Index* (*c*)
1938	31·3	31·3	31·3
1939	31·5	30·6	31·1
1940	34·3	27·7	29·1
1941	34·5	24·6	27·0
1942	35·8	23·9	27·9
1943	36·5	23·7	28·6
1944	38·2	24·3	29·6
1945	38·4	23·9	29·5
1946	41·4	25·1	31·7
1947	44·5	24·0	33·8

THE PRESENT STATE OF CO-OPERATIVE TRADE

Arrayed against the Co-operatives are the various private retail trading agencies—from large 'chains' of stores and big private department stores to the vast number of small shops, general or specialised, in both towns and villages. After a long period during which Co-operative trading steadily gained ground on its rivals by increasing its proportion of total retail trade, a stage seems now to have been reached at which neither appreciable relative gains nor losses are being made. The aggregate of Co-operative trade continues to grow, but certainly not more than in proportion to the total trade done by all kinds of agencies in the fields which the Co-operative movement actually attempts to cover. This means, in effect, that the Co-operative Societies' share in the total expenditure of its members is tending to fall; for, even apart from the effect of food subsidies in reducing the proportion of total income spent on food, consumers' expenditure has been shifting steadily as living standards have risen and as new wants have emerged. Many of the things on

TABLE VII

A Comparison between the Growth of Co-operative Retail Trade and that of Retail Trade as a Whole, as Measured by the Sample Statistics Collected by the Board of Trade, Covering about One-sixth of Total Retail Turnover

	Total Index		*Food Index*		*Non-food Index*	
	All Trade	*Co-op. Trade*	*All Trade*	*Co-op. Trade*	*All Trade*	*Co-op. Trade*
1942	100	100	100	100	100	100
1943	98	103	102	107	93	93
1944	105	109	107	113	101	99
1945	110	111	110	114	112	103
1946	130	126	123	126	142	126
1947	147	137	135	135	165	146
1948	167	153	151	149	192	176

Percentage Increases in Retail Sales, 1947–48 to 1948–49

	Department Stores	*Multiple Shops*	*Co-ops.*	*Total*
Food and Tobacco	2·6	13·8	11·6	12·0
Non-food . .	8·3	26·3	17·2	16·7
Total . . .	7·9	19·4	13·0	14·0

which consumers are spending more and more of their incomes fall wholly or mainly outside the range of present Co-operative services. The Co-operative Societies possess hardly any cinemas or theatres; they do not run garages or service stations; their restaurants are few, except in big towns, and nearly all unlicensed. They cater for holiday-making on only a small, though an increasing, scale; and, of course, they do not run football pools or greyhound racing tracks or public-houses.[1] They control a Sunday, but not a daily, newspaper, and their publishing and bookselling activities are as yet on a very small scale, and are

[1] Except the last in a very few cases.

TABLE VIII

An Analysis of Co-operative Retail Trade (Based on a Single Society)

	1937	1947	1948
Grocery and Tobacco	42·6	39·1	38·8
Bakery	9·5	7·9	7·9
Café	—	0·9	0·8
Butchering	10·9	6·4	4·8
Greengrocery	0·4	0·7	0·6
Fish and Poultry	—	1·1	1·4
Dairy	12·8	14·7	15·3
Total Food and Tobacco	76·3	71·0	69·6
Drapery	4·3	5·1	5·8
Boots	2·5	3·2	3·4
Tailoring	4·7	3·5	3·8
Furnishing	4·1	5·6	5·6
Total Dry Goods	15·7	17·5	18·6
Pharmacy	—	1·8	1·8
Coal	3·2	4·2	4·1
Other Departments	4·8	5·5	5·9

largely limited to printed matter of essentially Co-operative interest. Accordingly, however successful the Co-operative Societies might be in extending their connections within their traditional fields of trading activity, they could not expect to hold—much less to increase—the percentage of their members' total incomes attracted to the Co-operative Stores. Only by launching out upon a very wide range of new ventures, for which they possess at present neither the organisation nor the trained personnel, could they hope to offset the tendency for the average member to spend a falling proportion of his total income at the local 'Co-op.'. As the ordinary consumer comes to spend more of his income on services and less on shop goods, the Co-operative

TABLE IX

RETAIL CO-OPERATIVE SOCIETIES. CAPITAL, SURPLUS AND DIVIDEND RATES, 1938–48

	Share Capital £ million	*Loan Capital £ million*	*Total Capital £ million*	*Share Interest £ million*	*Net Surplus £ million*	*Surplus per £1 of Sales*	*Average Dividend*
1938 .	154·6	25·3	179·9	5·17	26·0	1/11¾	1/9¾
1939 .	157·6	25·9	183·5	5·20	26·8	1/11¾	1/9½
1940 .	156·4	25·1	181·5	5·23	27·8	1/10¼	1/7½
1941 .	164·4	26·4	190·8	5·27	28·9	1/11	1/8½
1942 .	179·5	28·8	208·3	5·51	33·1	2/1	1/10½
1943 .	201·0	33·1	234·2	6·02	33·8	2/0½	1/10
1944 .	222·3	38·6	260·9	6·55	35·2	2/0	1/9¾
1945 .	238·5	44·8	283·3	6·95	35·0	1/11¼	1/9
1946 .	247·2	50·8	298·0	7·05	38·2	1/10¾	1/8½
1947 .	248·2	55·7	303·9	6·91	40·0	1/9¾	1/7½
1948 .	244·7	60·4	305·1	6·63	40·1	1/7¼	1/5½
1949 .	238·5	62·6	301·1	6·38	42·0	1/6½	1/4½

Societies must lose ground unless they enter the 'services' field in a big way.

THE FINANCIAL ASPECTS OF CO-OPERATIVE DEVELOPMENT

Developments of this type, on a sufficient scale materially to alter the trend, would require a very big expenditure of capital, even if there were no other difficulties in the way. It is true that many of the local Societies have large capital reserves and also more share capital than they are using in their own trading ventures, and that they have at their back the credit resources of the Co-operative Wholesale Societies' Banking Departments, which are used largely outside the movement in short-term loans. Some students of Co-operation have suggested that the movement's financial resources are ample enough for much more considerable new capital investments than its leaders are at all prepared to consider. This is unquestionably true, though some of the estimates of the amount of free capital available in the movement have been very much exaggerated. There is a good mass of capital that could be invested in new ventures. But the leaders usually look on the matter in another light. The Co-operative movement is not only a great trading agency, but also a savings bank. Its share capital is accumulated mainly out of the dividends on purchases accruing to its members, and its loan stock out of members' small savings. In times of prosperity its capital resources pile up fast; but any serious economic setback is liable—though less than it was before the days of 'Social Security'—to lead to large withdrawals. Both share and loan capital in the Co-operative movement are liable to withdrawal at short notice; indeed, this facility of withdrawal was one of the main inducements to the working-class investor in the precarious days of the movement's growth. Co-operative capital resources, which piled up fast under the conditions of war-time scarcity and continued to pile up for some years after the war, now show some tendency to fall as they are drawn upon for arrears of household and other purchases or to meet, in some cases, increased living costs. There is still in the movement a large mass of capital that is not actually invested in Co-operative enterprise; but, say the leaders of the movement, the greater part of this needs to be kept liquid in view of possible large-scale withdrawals should there set in an economic crisis involving extensive unemployment or loss of earnings in the working-class households which account for the bulk of Co-operative membership.

It is, indeed, clear enough that the Co-operative movement, even if it is in a position to invest at a greater rate than is now practicable in face of shortages of man-power and supplies, could not, out of its existing capital resources or out of what it could expect to attract by existing methods, finance any really dramatic invasion of new fields of enterprise, or encroach on its rivals within its present range of activities at more than a moderate rate of growth. It could, for example, hardly make a really serious incursion into the film industry or attempt to become a great supplier of services to motorists on a scale comparable with its share in the trade in groceries or coal without tapping new sources of capital supply. Nor could it, even if the opportunity were to offer, afford to buy up its big rivals in the chain-store business, or in flour-milling, or in milk supply without resorting to essentially new methods of attracting capital. It does, no doubt, continually buy up rival businesses, including quite large department stores and small 'chains', as well as individual private shops; and it could to some extent intensify this process if more private businesses were to come into the market on attractive terms. It could not, however, within its present resources or means of increasing them, attempt in any of these fields action on a scale large enough to alter appreciably the total balance between Co-operative and other types of trade.[1]

THE ATTITUDE OF THE CO-OPERATIVE LEADERSHIP

Well aware of these limitations, most of the business leaders of the Co-operative movement take them for granted and pay little attention to idealistic notions of a 'Co-operative Commonwealth' in which Co-operation would have superseded all other methods of retail trading and would also have become the main producer at any rate of finished goods destined for the consumers' market. Co-operative managers, directors, and management committees for the most part carry on from year to year on the assumption that they will continue in competition with the various types of private enterprise and that the State will neither hamstring them by yielding altogether to the vociferous demands of private traders for measures against them nor, even when a Labour Government including Co-operative members is in power, set out to suppress or penalise their rivals for their benefit. The Co-operative leaders have grown up in an environment of steady and, on the whole, gratifying expansion; and, as long as this continues, they are under no strong inducement to think about longer-run problems or to philosophise about the proper functions of Co-operation in the society of the future. Nor do most of them do either of these things, even if they occasionally bring the 'Co-operative Commonwealth' into the peroration of a speech. Indeed, many of them hardly ever need to do even this: they are business men, running important and on the whole successful business concerns, according to the rules that have

[1] On this matter see further pages 58 ff.

been worked out for Co-operative enterprise over a century of experience, and, like the cobbler, they stick to their last. Most of them, indeed, are inclined, because of the conditions of their daily work, to a pretty conservative attitude towards business problems, as well as to a failure to consider at all the wider problems of a new social order.

This abstinence from speculation about the future is the easier because, as we have seen, the Co-operative movement tends to keep its trading activities and its idealism in separate, though not quite watertight, compartments. In its early days of struggle, before it had developed a professional managerial class of its own, trading activity and propaganda of Co-operation as a social ideal ran very closely together, and the same men managed the stores and made the speeches and dreamed of the future as complementary elements in a single cause. But nowadays at any rate the larger societies have their separate Managers or Trade Secretaries and Management Committees on the one hand, and Educational Secretaries and Educational Committees on the other; and thinking about Co-operative ideals and the 'Co-operative Commonwealth' is deemed to be mainly a function of the educational side—or of the Co-operative Party, which has grown up since 1917 into a third wing of the movement, largely distinct in active personnel from the other two. Discussions at party meetings or at educational conferences and schools about the 'Future of Co-operation' make very little impact on the trading side of the movement and have in practice not a great deal to do with its everyday commercial affairs. This, indeed, is an almost inevitable outcome of the movement's prodigious growth, which has enforced specialisation upon it and has attracted into its ranks a host of purchasing members who are not even mildly interested in Co-operation except as a convenient kind of shopping agency and perhaps as a handy means of saving up for large occasional expenses or for a 'rainy day'.

THE OUTLOOK FOR CONSUMERS' CO-OPERATION

In the light of what has been said, it seems unlikely that in the immediate future the Consumers' Co-operative movement will do more than hold its own in those fields of retail trade in which it is already actively engaged, or that it will make more than relatively small adventures into the supplying of consumers' wants for which it is not at present equipped to provide. Any attempt to extend at all rapidly its field of activity would inevitably involve trading risks beyond those which are involved in the traditional fields of Co-operative enterprise. The Co-operative movement has been built up hitherto largely on a basis of supplying everyday needs of working-class consumers, though in certain areas it also caters for the demand of a considerable number of middle-class consumers, especially for bread, milk, staple groceries, and coal. Its outstanding success has been in meeting a not highly diversified demand for a limited range of staple products, such as are bought in quantities not normally varying a great deal from week to week. The trade in such goods allows of a rapid turnover, does not require a large holding of stocks, and can be carried on with fairly low overhead expenses for advertisement or for the pushing of particular lines. The trade in these staples can carry a quite substantial trade in other goods, the demand for which is less standardised or less regular; but there are limits beyond which trade in these other kinds of goods cannot be carried without an increase of overheads and therewith in trading risks—at any rate, until the new techniques have been thoroughly learnt and the new forms of enterprise been developed on a big enough scale to carry their own risks. The spreading of dividends over the entire field, without specific allocation to particular types of trade, makes it possible for the Co-operative societies to strike out on ancillary branches of supply; and in some cases these other lines, while they are carried on in a selective way, can yield high surpluses. Nevertheless, any large-scale development of Co-operative retailing in fields involving a slower rate of turnover, the holding of larger diversified stocks, and the pushing of particular lines would be bound to increase the riskiness of Co-operative enterprise and accordingly to call for higher trading margins than at present prevail over the entire field of Co-operative trading—or alternatively for lower dividends on purchases.

TABLE X

CO-OPERATIVE DIVIDENDS

Average Rates of Dividend per £1 of Purchases from Retail Co-operative Societies in Great Britain, 1939 and 1943–49

	National Average	*Sectional Averages*							
		Scottish	*Northern*	*North-eastern*	*North-western*	*Midland*	*Southern*	*South-western*	*Western*
1939	1/9½	2/4	2/1	1/10¾	2/0¼	1/8½	1/2¼	1/5¼	1/5¼
1943	1/10	2/5½	2/2½	1/8¼	1/11	1/8	1/4¼	1/5¼	1/10¼
1944	1/9¾	2/5¾	2/3	1/8¼	1/10¼	1/7¾	1/3¼	1/5½	1/9½
1945	1/9	2/5¼	2/2¼	1/7¼	1/9½	1/7¼	1/2½	1/3½	1/9
1946	1/8½	2/4½	2/2	1/6¾	1/8¾	1/6½	1/2½	1/5	1/7¼
1947	1/7½	2/3½	2/2½	1/5	1/7½	1/5½	1/1½	1/3½	1/6½
1948	1/5½	2/0¾	2/0¼	1/3	1/5¼	1/3½	1/0	1/1¼	1/4½
1949	1/4½	1/11	1/11	1/2½	1/3¾	1/2¾	11¾	1/0½	1/3½

PRICES AND DIVIDENDS

Already there has been, in recent years, a quite marked tendency for the average rates of dividend on purchases to fall. This is partly because the very high dividends which used to be paid by many societies in the industrial areas—particularly the coalfields—had to be reduced during the inter-war period in order to meet the worsened circumstances of members in depressed industries and areas. There is no doubt that in a considerable number of areas before 1914 Co-operative prices were well above the prices of competitive private traders, and could be so for the reason that consumers consciously used the Co-operative Society as a savings bank and preferred high prices with high dividends to lower prices with lower dividends because they wished to use the dividend as a means of saving. This situation largely disappeared between the wars, and *average* Co-operative dividends fell off. The South of England and other areas where Co-operation was relatively weak were not greatly affected, because the keenness of competition between Co-

TABLE XI

RETAIL CO-OPERATIVE SOCIETIES, 1912 AND 1937–49

Surplus as Percentage of Retail Sales (after deduction of Interest)

	National Average (incl. Ireland)	*Scotland*	*Northern*	*North-eastern*	*North-western*	*Midland*	*Southern*	*South-western*	*Western*
1912	13·4	16·1	14·9	14·1		10·4	8·0	8·8	11·4
1937	9·86	12·97	10·67	9·70	10·90	9·45	7·55	7·41	8·79
1938	9·87	12·51	10·90	10·19	11·01	9·58	7·39	7·66	8·93
1939	9·85	12·29	11·00	10·11	10·89	9·85	7·33	7·86	9·07
1940	9·31	11·57	10·62	9·35	10·08	9·40	6·74	7·74	9·23
1941	9·56	12·55	10·45	9·03	10·07	9·43	6·80	8·14	10·30
1942	10·37	13·62	11·51	9·28	10·60	9·95	8·08	9·09	10·63
1943	10·19	13·16	11·47	9·40	10·43	9·67	8·19	8·46	9·85
1944	10·00	13·14	11·66	9·26	10·02	9·51	7·81	8·48	9·44
1945	9·76	12·91	11·49	8·98	9·96	9·08	7·59	8·32	9·08
1946	9·55	12·98	11·56	8·73	9·42	8·95	7·28	8·44	8·73
1947	9·07	12·37	11·63	7·99	8·90	8·50	6·84	7·47	8·30
1948	8·03	11·16	10·48	7·03	7·80	7·49	6·00	6·32	7·32
1949	7·70	10·43	10·09	6·95	7·25	7·24	5·97	5·83	7·09

operative and private traders had never allowed really high dividends to be paid. In these areas the Co-operative Societies could seldom afford to charge more than the market prices charged by competitive private traders, and relatively low dividends corresponding to normal private trading net profits were much more the rule. In 1948–49, when the Co-operatives made an attempt to extend their trade by deliberate price-cutting, at a time when the Labour Government was pleading for measures to keep down the cost of living, it became speedily apparent that the societies, at any rate in the areas in which private competition was strong, could not reduce prices without direct repercussions on rates of dividend on purchases, and that a good many Co-operators positively preferred standard prices with customary rates of dividend to lower prices at the cost of sharp falls in dividend rates. The savings bank element in Co-operative trading remains important, even though the vast majority of Co-operators now prefer a moderate dividend to a higher dividend inflated by selling prices set at an artificially high level.

INTEREST RATES

Dividend of course depends on the rate of interest payable on share and loan capital, as well as on the prices charged for goods in the Co-operative Stores. Co-operative rates of interest have tended, with some time-lag, to follow the movement of long-term interest rates in general—especially rates of interest on Government bonds. Any large increase in Co-operative share or loan capital could be brought about, if at all, only by offering higher returns than are available elsewhere on capital withdrawable at short notice—e.g. capital invested in Building Societies; and should there be a sustained rise in long-term rates of interest generally, the Co-operative Societies would probably have to follow suit unless they were prepared to face substantial withdrawals of funds. Considerable capital expansion would inevitably involve the offer of higher interest rates than would need to be paid if the movement were content with a slower pace of advance; and the necessity of paying more for additional capital would increase costs for capital already invested in the movement, and would thus tend to react on the size of the trading surplus, and on the rate of dividend that could be afforded on purchases at any given level of selling prices. No doubt, in the long run the economies that could be achieved by means of large-scale handling of the new kinds of trade might amply suffice to cover these additional costs—given really skilled and enterprising management. But in the short run I think this would be too much to expect; and it is of the short run that Co-operative managers and committee-men think mainly in deciding what forms of development to attempt. Co-operative management suffers to-day from an excessive timidity which is by no means all the managers' fault. The managers have to account for their doings and projects to committees and Members' Meetings that are influenced very much more by the fear of even a small fall in next year's dividend than by even large prospects of long-run gains through the conquest of new fields of enterprise.

CO-OPERATIVE TRADE AND CO-OPERATIVE PRODUCTION

In these circumstances, the Co-operative sector of retail trade does not appear likely to advance very rapidly as the outcome of a continuance of the existing forms of competition between Co-operative and private enterprise—at any rate, unless Co-operative efficiency can be advanced at a pace well in excess of the improvement in private trading methods. There is certainly no present sign that even in the longest run Co-operative trading will supersede, or even seriously encroach on, private trade, even within the fields in which it has been most successful hitherto. The notion that the inherent superiority of Co-operative trading methods will enable the Co-operative societies, within any measurable span of years, to achieve a *de facto* monopoly, even within a limited field, by sheer competitive superiority, finds no warrant in the results of an objective study of current trends in retailing.

Broadly speaking, the scope for the expansion of Co-operative activity in wholesale trading is limited by the development of Co-operative retail trade. The local Co-operative societies already buy the bulk of their supplies, beyond what they produce for themselves, through the Wholesale Societies, which they jointly own; and the growth of wholesale trade is accordingly bound to depend mainly on the expansion of retail sales. The position is not quite the same in respect of Co-operative production, which is carried on mainly by the Wholesale Societies, though retail and federal societies also make a considerable contribution, and account has to be taken of the activities of the Producers' Societies organised in the Co-operative Productive Federation[1] and of the small band of Agricultural Societies engaged in Co-operative marketing.[2] In the manufacturing field, there is room for a considerable expansion of Co-operative activity, even without a proportionate growth in the volume of Co-operative

[1] See Chapters IX and X. [2] See pages 109 ff.

retail trade. But here again the pace of expansion depends on the availability of capital, as well as on the ability to secure both licences for building and equipment and the man-power needed for new productive enterprises. Nor can it be questioned that any rapid expansion of Co-operative manufacture, out of step with the growth of retail demand, would involve increased risks, through the resort to less standardised and more diversified forms of production. In this field, too, it is quite unrealistic to look forward to any rate of growth that would encroach seriously on the private-enterprise sector of the national economy merely as a result of a continuance and intensification of the existing trends.

CO-OPERATIVE ATTITUDES FURTHER CONSIDERED

In all these circumstances, the attitude of the main body of the leaders of the Co-operative movement, on its trading side, comes near to an acceptance of the continuance for an altogether indefinite period of Co-operative trading side by side with private trading and in competition with it—that is, to an acceptance for an indefinite time to come of something not very different from the *status quo*; though of course hopes are expressed that there will be a continuous encroachment by the Co-operative movement on the sphere of private trade, at any rate within the fields in which Co-operation has already established its position. Co-operators are for the most part much more intent on holding what they have, and on preserving their right to expand gradually in competition with their rivals, than on staking out new claims which would require the adoption of radically new methods or involve invoking the positive assistance of the State on their side with the object of ousting their competitors from any part of the field.

THE VOLUNTARY PRINCIPLE

This attitude is the stronger because Co-operators have from the very beginning been proud of the essentially *voluntary* character of their movement. They have appealed to consumers to trade at their stores and to become shareholding members with a mixture of appeals to idealism and morality and to self-interest. Mutual trading has been held out as at one and the same time morally superior to profit-making and more advantageous to the consumer from the economic standpoint; and the effect of Co-operation in encouraging thrift and in discouraging credit trading has also been strongly emphasised. It was among the thriftier and more regularly employed sections of the working classes, much more than among the casuals, the bottom dogs and the improvident, that Consumers' Co-operation made its converts; and the movement has always been to some extent *selective*, just as the Trade Unions have been, and has tended to represent a section, rather than the whole, of the working-class consumers. This selectiveness has been much less in evidence in recent years, because of the considerable rise in the relative economic position of the less skilled and less well-paid workers. But it remains: the Co-operative movement is still, not only a *voluntary* movement which no one need join unless he wishes, but also a movement much more adapted to the needs of the higher than of the lower strata of the working classes. It would need to alter its methods considerably in order to bring in, not merely as members but as regular purchasers of a wide range of goods, the entire working class; and it is doubtful whether most of its leaders would at all relish the changes that would have to be introduced for this purpose. For the attraction of the poorer consumers who are now, wholly or mainly, supplying their requirements from non-Co-operative sources would involve a heavy capital expenditure far beyond what the new recruits could be expected to meet through investments in share or loan capital—even if it did not involve in addition both a great extension of credit trading and higher overheads on account of sales in smaller quantities and of inferior qualities of goods. However richly such ventures might turn out in the long run, it cannot be easy to persuade a Quarterly Meeting concerned mainly with immediate dividends to sanction the heavy capital expenditure and the prospective rises in immediate costs which many of them involve.

At one time, the struggle against adulteration played an

important part in establishing the Co-operative movement's appeal in competition with private traders. Nowadays, thanks to the public enforcement of minimum standards of purity and genuineness in retail trade as a whole, this factor is much less important than it used to be. But it still retains some importance; and the Co-operator of to-day does not look to the Stores either for exceptional bargains or for inferior goods at correspondingly low prices. The voluntarism which Co-operators still acclaim as the basis of their movement has in it a strong economic, as well as some idealistic, element. It is not only that no one need become a Co-operator unless he, or she, wishes to: it is also that the movement does not, in general, put itself out to cater for those sections of the consuming public that are likely to be, economically considered, more trouble than they are worth.

Thus, if the Co-operative leaders were invited to make the local Consumers' Societies the sole retail agency for the supply of the kinds of goods which they already market on a considerable scale, it is unlikely that they would receive the proposal with much enthusiasm, even on purely economic grounds. Their response might be more favourable if they were asked to take over only a particular trade for which they have shown special aptitude, and in which the advantages of monopoly have clear economic attractions—say, the retail supply of milk or coal in towns in which they are already well equipped and are supplying a high proportion of the total demand. But even such an offer would probably be met with a certain hesitation, because it would destroy, though only within a limited field, the *voluntary* basis of Co-operative membership.

This question of voluntarism is indeed of crucial significance. When Co-operative idealists talk of the 'Co-operative Commonwealth', they can envisage their movement as having developed, at some distant date, into a universal supplier to which every consumer is attached as a matter of course, and to contemplate a situation in which private trade has been driven wholly from the field by the superior economic and moral merits of Co-operative mutual trading. In such visions, voluntarism can be seen as having become consistent with monopoly because everyone has

TABLE XII

An Index of Co-operative Retail Prices, 1934–48

(Main foods, soap and coal only)

1934 = 100, *compared with Ministry of Labour Food and Cost of Living Indexes converted to the same basis.*

	Old Co-op. Index		*Min. of Labour Index*		*New Co-op. Index* based on White Paper Price Estimates (1938 = 100)*	
	General	*Food only*	*Cost of Living*	*Food only*	*General*	*Food and Tobacco*
1934	100·0	—	100	100		
1935	104·2	—	101	102		
1936	109·3	—	104	107		
1937	116·4	—	109	114		
1938	117·5	—	111	115	100	100
1939	119·9	—	112	116	103	104
1940	137·6	—	130	134	124	123
1941	141·0	—	141	138	140	133
1942	138·1	—	142	132	150	141
1943	144·5	—	141	136	154	147
1944	148·8	—	142	138	157	149
1945	150·5	—	144	139	161	151
1946	151·4	148·6	144	138	165	153
1947	152·5	147·7	144 (June)	132 (June)	185	177
1948 (11 mths.)	162·3	154·8	—	—	—	—

* From *Co-operative Review*, January 1949.

chosen the same thing. But when it is a matter, not of Utopia, but of practical and immediate policy, voluntarism and monopoly cannot be made consistent. The one or the other has to be sacrificed; and it has to be admitted that voluntarism involves the continuance of alternative forms of trade—that is, in practice, a survival of private suppliers as the competitors of the Co-operative societies—unless, indeed, it is envisaged that their place is to be filled by some form of State or municipal trading in direct competition with the Co-operative movement. As we have seen, the nature of the Co-operative reaction to this last notion was left in no doubt when in 1949 a minor Labour minister—Lord Shepherd—incautiously dropped a few words which hinted at a possible entry of the State into the sphere of retail trade.

TABLE XIII

RETAIL CO-OPERATIVE TRADE, EXPENSES AND SURPLUSES (BASED ON A SINGLE SOCIETY)

The figures represent the percentage share of each Branch in the total of trade expenses and net surpluses respectively

	Percentage Share in		
	(*a*) *Trade*	(*b*) *Distributive Expenses*	(*c*) *Net Surplus*
Grocery and Tobacco	38·8	30·9	21·6
Bakery	7·9	7·5	17·5
Café	0·8	2·1	2·0
Butchering	4·8	5·2	9·2
Greengrocery	0·6	0·5	1·1
Fish and Poultry	1·4	1·3	0·8
Dairy	15·3	24·7	10·7
Total Food and Tobacco	69·6	72·3	60·8
Drapery	5·8	5·8	8·3
Boots	3·4	3·0	7·0
Tailoring	3·8	4·1	4·9
Furnishing	5·6	5·5	6·9
Total Dry Goods	18·6	18·4	27·1
Pharmacy	1·8	1·7	2·2
Coal	4·1	4·6	3·8
Other Departments	5·9	2·9	6·0

Chapter IV

CO-OPERATIVE RESOURCES–MAN-POWER AND DISTRIBUTION

*

At present it is the usual practice for anyone who makes more than a few casual purchases at a Co-operative Store to become a member and to acquire a shareholding interest as well as a right to receive dividends on purchases. Or rather, this is true of households. There is great variation from district to district in the practice in respect of individual membership. In some cases, husband, wife, and grown-up children are all members; in others, only the husband is a shareholding member, even if the wife makes most of the purchases. The tendency has been in the direction of family membership, but I do not know of any statistics showing either nationally or locally how many separate households the aggregate membership represents.

At the end of 1948 the share capital held by members averaged £24, as compared with £18 in 1939 and £15 in 1914. It has thus tended to fall in real value, and there has been some decline since 1945, when the average was £25 10*s*. If loan capital at about £6 a head is added to share capital, the Co-operative member had on the average in 1948 an investment of £30 in his or her local Society.

Averages are, however, in this matter grossly misleading. I know of no up-to-date figures showing how these capital holdings are distributed; but in 1932 less than one-third of the total number of members held as much as £3, as against an average of £16, and the lowest third of the membership held less than £1 10*s*. Only 12 per cent. held more than £25. Thus the bulk of Co-operative capital was owned by a small fraction of the members; and the rapid growth of membership since the date of this analysis is likely to have accentuated this concentration, both because new members tend to hold less than old and because the development of family membership tends to mean an addition of members holding only a small capital investment.

The tendency towards a decline in the real value of average capital holdings is, however, due also to another factor—the great increase in alternative openings for the investment of working-class savings. The capital invested in Building Societies has risen from £62 millions in 1913 to £2,815 millions in 1948. Industrial Insurance Company life premiums have increased over the same period from £17 millions to well over £90 millions; and there have been smaller, but very considerable, increases in the premium income of Friendly and Collecting Societies. The State, with its National Savings movement, has become a further competitor for the savings of the working classes. Of course, not all these huge sums by a long way have come out of working-class savings. But enough have to reduce very greatly the proportion of such savings flowing into Co-operative channels.

Nevertheless, Co-operative capital is still largely in excess of what is needed to finance Co-operative trade and production at the existing levels. The local Consumers' Societies, through which capital mainly flows into the movement, need only a fraction of their resources to finance their own operations. In 1948, out of total capital resources of £398 millions, the local Societies had no less than £270 millions invested outside their own internal holdings of fixed and working capital. These investments were distributed as shown in Table XIV, p. 60.

Thus more than two-thirds of the total investments were in the Wholesale Societies, and three-quarters in other Co-operative Societies, leaving one-quarter, or nearly £69 millions, invested outside the Co-operative movement, mainly in public securities.

The total assets of the local Consumers' Societies were made up as shown in Table XV, p. 61.

Thus fixed capital and stocks of goods absorb only about a quarter of the local Societies' capital, and investments account for more than two-thirds of the total. But the major part of the investments, placed in the hands of the Wholesale Societies, is used to finance Co-operative enterprise, including not only

TABLE XIV

Investments Held by Local Consumers' Societies

(£ millions)

	1939	*Per cent.*	1946	*Per cent.*	1948	*Per cent.*
In the Wholesale Societies	95·9	67·5	196·0	69·8	181·5	67·2
In other Co-operative Societies* . . .	4·6	3·25	7·4	2·6	8·9	3·3
In the Co-operative Building Society . .	7·3	5·2	8·6	3·1	10·0	4·1
In other Building Societies	0·2	0·1	0·1	0·05	0·2	0·07
In British and Colonial Government Stock .	3·6	2·6	38·1	13·6	38·2	14·1
In Local Authority and Public Board Stock .	16·8	11·8	21·4	7·6	19·5	7·2
In Joint Stock Companies	0·7	0·5	0·7	0·25	1·1	0·4
In Advances to Members .	13·0	9·1	8·5	3·0	9·8	3·6
	142·2	100	208·8	100	270·3	100

* Federal, Productive and Agricultural.

wholesale trade and production, but also banking and insurance facilities for the local Societies.

The Wholesale Societies draw most of their capital from the local Consumers' Societies, which look to them for dividends on their purchases as well as for interest. The assets of the Wholesale Societies are made up as shown in Table XVI, p. 61.

These totals, however, include the assets of the C.W.S. and S.C.W.S. Banks, which are carried on as departments of the Wholesale Societies. The C.W.S. carries its trade credits to local Societies in its Banking Department, whereas the S.C.W.S. includes them in its Trading Department. The figures are thus not wholly comparable; and they also give an inflated impression of the capital position of the C.W.S. as a trading body. The position can be seen more clearly when the capital and liabilities are set beside the assets. (See Table XVII.)

TABLE XV

ASSETS OF LOCAL CONSUMERS' SOCIETIES

	Amount, £ millions		*Percentage*	
	1946	1948	1946	1948
Property	55·0	63·5	14·42	15·94
Stocks of Goods	26·6	45·1	6·98	11·31
Investments	280·8	270·3	73·60	67·82
Members' Debts	5·5	10·1	1·43	2·54
Cash in Hand	11·5	7·0	3·02	1·75
Sundry Assets	2·1	2·5	0·55	0·64
	381·5	398·5	100	100

TABLE XVI

ASSETS OF C.W.S. AND S.C.W.S., 1948

(*£ thousands*)

	Property	*Stock-in-trade*	*Invest-ments*	*Debtors*	*Cash*	*Misc.*	*Total*
C.W.S.	10,891	17,867	228,856	15,201	22,726	1,195	296,736
S.C.W.S.	3,432	4,584	13,264	4,287	782	—	26,349
	14,323	22,451	242,120	19,488	23,508	1,195	323,085

TABLE XVII

CAPITAL AND LIABILITIES OF C.W.S. AND S.C.W.S., 1948

(*£ millions*)

	Capital		*Reserves and Insurance Funds*	*Sundry Liabilities*	*Dispens-able Balance*	*Sundry Funds and Overdrafts*
	Share	*Loan*				
C.W.S.	20,144	143,992	19,010	13,323	4,061	96,207
S.C.W.S.	2,312	17,686	3,529	2,090	494	238
	22,456	161,678	22,539	15,413	4,555	96,445

It will be seen that the Wholesale Societies are financed mainly by loan capital, most of which comes from the local Consumers' Societies. Total share and loan capital amounts to £184 millions, which is only a little more than the investment held by the local Societies. £96 millions of the total assets is accounted for by the 'Sundry Funds', which are mainly holdings of the C.W.S. Bank. If this is deducted, there remains a total of £146 millions held in investments, partly as the working capital of the two Banks but partly as a surplus of assets available for Co-operative development. This sum, however, includes the investments of the Wholesale Societies in other Co-operative undertakings, and is by no means all 'free' money available for new development. Nevertheless, there remains a large sum that could be so invested, at some cost in liquidity, but, as far as can be seen, without leaving the Wholesale Societies at all short of working capital or unable to face the considerable withdrawals of loan capital that might occur in a recession. There was actually some withdrawal of loan capital between 1945 and 1948. Over these three years, whereas share capital rose by £1·4 millions, loan capital fell by £6 millions, as a result of withdrawals for post-war spending. But clearly the Wholesales could stand a very much greater drain than this without any risk of running short of liquid resources. They could afford, as far as capital resources go, to expand a lot faster than they show any signs of wishing to expand at present.

The average capital investment of £30 a member, then, is more than enough to sustain the present activities of the movement, including the Wholesale, Federal and Productive Societies as well as the local Consumers' Societies. It allows room for substantial expansion along the present lines, but not for dramatic new developments, such as the taking over of a greatly increased proportion of either total retail trade or production. Accordingly, if any large amount of existing retail trade now in private hands were to be taken over by Co-operative agencies, a large part of the capital for the conduct of the increased Co-operative business would have to be provided from outside the present Co-operative movement.

Thus the question of the development of Co-operative trade is closely bound up with the much wider question of the future of retail trading as a whole, and, accordingly, also with the future of a large section of wholesale trade. It will be most convenient to begin, in this chapter, with the problem of retailing, and to come later to the more specialised problems of the various branches of wholesale trade.

MAN-POWER IN DISTRIBUTION

Before, however, we set out to consider the future of retailing, we are confronted with the wider issue of the amount of man-power which Great Britain can afford in its present situation to devote to the distributive industry as a whole. From the national standpoint, it is of the greatest importance, in view of the present and prospective balance of payments, to avoid as far as possible any *waste* of man-power in supplying the home consumers' needs, both in order to make the most of limited resources of man-power in meeting these needs to the satisfaction of the consumers and in order to release resources of man-power for producing additional exports to pay for necessary imports. Of course, waste of man-power is no more objectionable in retail trade than in any other occupation; but there is a widespread feeling that, in relation to our total resources, we are using as a nation more labour than we can reasonably spare in the distributive and allied trades. These trades, according to the latest available figures, were in July 1949 using the services of 2,771,000 persons out of a total working population of 23,205,000—that is, nearly 12 per cent., or 12½ per cent. of the total number in *civil* employment, leaving out the armed forces. Out of this total of 2,771,000, the insured workers in the distributive trades accounted for 2,219,000, of whom at least 1,600,000 were employed in retail distribution and the rest in various forms of wholesale trade. This leaves about 550,000 to be accounted for as shopkeepers or employers outside the range of unemployment insurance. It is unfortunately not possible to compare these figures with those for earlier dates, owing to changes in the method of compiling statistics of man-power. The Census of

1931 showed about 3 million persons occupied in the distributive trades, wholesale and retail, and of these nearly 2 million were classified as 'operatives', and the rest as employers, managers or persons working on their own account. The total working force in 1931 was about 21 million; so that the distributive trades then occupied over 14 per cent. of the total working population, as against 12 per cent. to-day. There has been some fall, both absolute and relative, largely as a result of the sharp contraction that was brought about during the years of war. The figures compiled by the Ministry of Labour show a decline of total man-power employed in the distributive trades from 2,887,000 in June 1939 to 1,927,000 in June 1944, followed by a recovery to 2,319,000 in June 1947. The revised figures show 2,689,000 for June 1948 and 2,766,000 for June 1949. Thus the distributive trades are still increasing their total man-power, but are still below the pre-war figures—which, however, included a substantial number of unemployed workers (224,000 in 1931, by the Census figures, and 179,000 in 1938, by the Ministry of Labour returns).

Out of the total of 2,271,000 persons employed in distribution, the retail Co-operative Societies employed about 218,000 and the Wholesale Societies another 12,500—but these figures include transport workers employed by the retail societies. Allowing for this, Co-operative employment in distribution is probably about 9 per cent. of the total man-power engaged in that service. It is hardly possible to say how closely this corresponds to the percentage of total trade that is in Co-operative hands; but about 10 per cent. is probably a fair estimate, as on the average the Co-operative employee probably handles a slightly larger turnover in actual goods, especially when allowance is made for the effect of subsidies in depressing the money value of trade in food as against other forms of retail and wholesale trading.

There is, of course, no way of saying categorically how large a proportion of its man-power a country can usefully, or can afford to, devote to the service of distribution. The tendency for the proportion of persons engaged in what is called 'tertiary employment'—that is, services, as against agriculture, mining and manufacture—to increase with advancing wealth and standards of living is well known, and is borne out by the experience of many countries. Were it not for Great Britain's exceptional position, with a total labour force at best stationary and tending to fall, and a highly exceptional dependence on overseas trade, it might be held that an expansion of the distributive trades at least to the pre-war level of employment was fully justified. But, as matters stand, there are strong reasons for economising in man-power to the fullest practicable extent in every occupation; and the additional productive workers who are needed in the export industries can be drawn only from other occupations, among which distribution is much the largest user of man-power. It is therefore unavoidable that consideration should be given, not only to such possible economies as the development of self-service shops, on which the Co-operative movement has already made a fairly promising start, but also to the possible means of preventing an undue increase in the number of shops.

STARTING NEW SHOPS

This factor has been recently under fairly severe control on account of the requirement to obtain a licence from the local authority, as well as of the restrictions on the building of new shops. These controls were, however, meant to be temporary, and nothing has yet been decided about the forms of control, if any, that are to be applied in the future. Co-operators frequently allege that they have been unfairly treated by many local authorities when they have applied for licences in competition with private traders; and this complaint is undoubtedly justified in certain areas, and has been an important factor in driving the Co-operative societies to buy up private businesses, where they have been able to, in order to extend their trade. Co-operative experience in competing for licences has been an important factor in strengthening Co-operators' opposition to any proposal for permanent licensing of shops, designed to keep their number down to what is really needed for efficient service of the public. Co-operators are rightly suspicious that any such system would either be operated unfairly against them in many areas or, at best, would tend to stabilise the existing shares of Co-operative and private retail agencies in the trades concerned, and would thus stand formidably in the way of development both in existing and in new fields of Co-operative enterprise.

THE CASE AGAINST LICENSING RESTRICTIONS

Quite apart from Co-operative objections, any general system of licensing retail outlets, in order to prevent an excess of shops, would be liable to create a series of dangerous monopolies in the retail trades and to facilitate agreements for price maintenance, and, perhaps, restriction of services, in the interests of private profit. The better way of restricting the number of shops, when it threatens to become excessive, is by regulation of prices so as to limit retail trading margins and thus make it less advantageous to set up unnecessary shops. There was a tendency between the wars for the number of shops to grow, as new ones were set up in areas in which population was increasing much more rapidly than old ones were closed in areas of declining population. War conditions helped to counteract this tendency, both because of the check to new building and because many existing shops were blitzed or had to close down. Demobilisation naturally brought with it a desire both to start up again many closed businesses and to found new ones; but, as we have seen, these tendencies have been held to some extent in check by the shortage of building facilities, and there have been special restrictions on the opening of new shops. In the food trades especially, where wholesaling has been largely in the hands of the Ministry of Food and prices have been under regulation for many commodities, retail margins have been kept within bounds for controlled goods; but the margins have been in most cases big enough, in view of rapid turnover and the absence of bad debts and wastage of unsold goods, to allow high profits to be made even by traders who are no more than moderately efficient. The removal of controls over prices would therefore probably stimulate the establishment of many new shops if the obstacles were removed; and a considerable waste of man-power could be avoided, if it became easier to open new shops, only by considerably tighter regulation of prices and trading margins. Under these conditions, the Co-operatives would be free to extend their business in free competition with other forms of retail trade.

TYPES OF PRIVATE SHOP

There is, however, no real prospect that this renewal of competition, even if it were accompanied by drastic action against retail trade agreements for price maintenance, would enable the Co-operative Societies to supersede private trading, or even to make rapid inroads on the business of their major rivals. These fall mainly into five groups—the private chain stores, the large department stores, the larger independent shops confined to a single line or to a few related lines, the small urban or suburban shops, and the type of 'general shop' found in many villages. Of these, only the first and second belong to the sphere of large-scale capitalist enterprise; and some of the smaller chains and department stores are more analogous to small-scale manufacturing businesses than to large capitalist concerns. The Trade Unions are apt to take objection to the third, fourth and fifth groups, because their employees, when they have any outside the owner's family, are very difficult to organise, and because they are apt to give worse wages and conditions than the larger distributive concerns. It can, however, hardly be denied that the small private shop serves in many cases a very useful social purpose, which the Co-operative Societies are by no means in a position to replace. The general village shop, the 'shop just round the corner' in town or suburb, and the specialised shop selling goods in the choice of which skill and taste play a large part, are all desirable elements in the total provision for the consumer and, given no undue multiplication in their numbers, unobjectionable from a social point of view, provided that they are compelled by law to observe proper minimum conditions of employment. On the other hand, Socialists can hardly contemplate the indefinite continuance of large capitalistic concerns in retail trade, or wait for those Greek Kalends when the Co-operative Societies will have driven them out of business by the sheer force of voluntary competition. The supersession of large-scale capitalist enterprise in retail distribution is not a task that should be given any high priority in the Socialist programme. For some time to come, it will be enough to establish an effective control over prices and margins and to prevent restrictive forms of price maintenance and cartellisation. But in the longer run it will be necessary to devise methods for the elimination of large-scale capitalism from retail distribution; and, though this need still lies some way ahead, it is desirable to consider the problem now, because unless it is thought out it will be impossible to arrive at any clear idea of the place of consumers' Co-operation in the coming Socialist society.

THE FUTURE OF SMALL SHOPS

I am accordingly assuming in what follows that nothing will be done to interfere with the continuance of the small shopkeeper as far as he is able to hold his own in fair competition with larger-scale enterprise. He is likely to be able to do this much more in some trades than in others, and for some time much more in villages and certain suburban areas than in large towns. His most useful services are performed either by providing a convenient shop close to the housewife's doorstep, at some distance from a main shopping centre, or by undertaking some kind of special service in which personal attention or skill in the choice of stocks to suit particular tastes or in the carrying out of repairs and special jobs for individual customers gives him a personal advantage. I can see no good reason why it should be thought desirable to supersede small traders of any of these types, provided only that, in as far as they employ hired labour, they conform to satisfactory standards of wages and conditions—and of course provided also that they obey the regulations laid down for shopkeepers in general in the areas concerned.

If, however, small shopkeepers are to survive—as I believe they should in a number of fields—their position will be greatly altered by changes in the structure of wholesale trade. If, as I shall suggest later, wholesaling passes mainly into the hands of State or Co-operative, or of joint State and Co-operative, agencies, the small retailer will be drawing the bulk of his supplies from such bodies, and not from profit-making traders or manufacturers. Under such conditions, the small traders will either deal individually with the 'socialised' big wholesalers, or will need to form mutual associations of their own for collective buying, or at any rate for collective negotiation of the terms of purchase. In this country, and on a larger scale in other countries, there have already been numerous instances of Co-operative Societies formed by groups of small traders for this purpose, or for the collective provision of credit; and bodies of this kind may come to be needed in many more cases. It is, however, a moot point whether the small traders will best serve the public by setting up their own Co-operative agencies, or by securing representation on, and special negotiating arrangements with, the general public and Co-operative bodies handling the bulk of wholesale trade.[1]

[1] For the discussion of the future of wholesale trade as a whole, see Chapters VII and VIII.

Chapter V

THE SOCIALISATION OF RETAIL TRADE

*

BEFORE I go on to discuss the future organisation of the distributive trades in a Socialist Britain and the place of the Co-operative movement in this organisation, I had better try to set down, as clearly as I can in a very short space, what I have in mind as the essential characteristics of the Socialist society to which I am looking forward. I am envisaging, not any sort of Socialist Utopia, and certainly not any kind of society in which all economic activities will have passed into the hands of the State, but rather the kind of structure that might be reached at the end of a generation of socialistic development under a series of Governments democratically responsible to the electorate and setting out to work with rather than against the grain of the British democratic tradition.

In the society which I envisage there will have been a great reduction in the inequality of capital ownership, as well as of incomes. Large inherited fortunes, I assume, will have been wiped out by taxation on some variant of the Rignano plan, under which large properties pass to the State at the death of the owner, subject to annuity charges for descendants for one or more lives. Accordingly, the provision of capital for investment will have ceased to depend at all on wealthy individuals, and will have come to depend, as it does to a great extent already, on the accumulation of business reserves in enterprises publicly or privately owned, on small savings by wage and salary earners, and on State investment out of budgetary funds. The ownership of a large fraction of industrial capital will have passed into public hands, not only by socialisation of particular industries or enterprises, but also by the surrender of capital holdings in payment of taxes on inheritance. Private enterprise will need to be financed largely by advances of capital from public sources, except where it is on a small scale; and small savings will flow chiefly into Co-operative enterprises, or be canalised through Building Societies and insurance agencies into projects of recognised public importance.

In such a social system there will be room for many diverse forms of economic enterprise. Some additional industries will no doubt have been nationalised outright and placed under the control either of National Boards more democratically constituted than those which have been set up so far or of some other kind of public authority. Some key enterprises, as distinct from whole industries, will also have been taken over and transferred to public management. In basic industries left mainly unnationalised, there will be representative Development Boards, set up by statute, with wide functions of economic planning and control within the general directives of a major economic plan laid down by Government subject to parliamentary sanction. In these industries, in addition to some nationalised enterprises, there will be many firms in which the public is directly interested either on account of capital loans to aid development or through the holding of shares surrendered in payment of inheritance taxes. In the industries producing mainly for the consumers' market, and perhaps in others, there will be a substantial Co-operative sector, including Producers' Co-operative Societies as well as establishments owned by the Consumers' Societies. There will still be opportunity to start and develop private businesses; but the scarcity of private capital will make it necessary for public agencies to stand ready to help promising ventures with advances of capital—for example, by providing buildings to rent on publicly owned Industrial Trading Estates, and by loans through special Finance Corporations such as already exist on a small scale. All these varied forms of enterprise will be operating within the framework of a general system of economic planning designed both to keep the level of investment reasonably steady and to guide capital into the forms of enterprise most needed in the national interest and, in their structure, most in accord with the requirements of industrial democracy.

I know that this sketch of the type of society I have in mind is very crude and can give only the most rudimentary notion of the reality behind the framework. But in order to be more specific I should have to write a whole book about the structure of the coming society in Great Britain; whereas in this book I am seeking to cover only a small part of this immense field. I can therefore say no more now about these general postulates concerning the economic structure; but there are a few words to be added about the social atmosphere in which these new economic institutions will be growing up. As the new society will—if my anticipations are at all near correctness—be much less class divided than the society of to-day, its dependence on the quality of its ordinary citizens and on an improved quality of democratic leadership will be much intensified. It will have to rely much more on the ordinary man's capacity for self-government and co-operative organisation, and on the emergence of leaders and organisers from the body of the people. It will have to take measures to spot the potential leaders, to provide diversified forms of training for leadership in every field, and to create a devoted body of public-spirited enthusiasts, fired by a common sense of mission, who will work together in its service, unifying their dispersed activities by reference to a common aim and to a common Socialist ideal.

Without this leadership, the new society at which the Labour and Co-operative Parties—indeed, all sections of the working-class movement—profess to be aiming simply cannot be realised at all. It is impossible to make either democratic Socialism or the 'Co-operative Commonwealth', or any fusion of the two, a reality without getting the key positions manned by ardent believers in Socialist and Co-operative ideals, or without the aid of a widely diffused body of adherents to act as leaders of public opinion in every field of social activity, from the workshop to the 'neighbourhood group', which is coming more and more to be recognised as the key factor in the development of civic consciousness and democratic social organisation. It falls quite beyond the scope of this book to discuss the ways and means of creating this pervasive spirit of democracy and the new forms of leadership that are indispensable for its growth. But it needs to be pointed out that, in the absence of these things, neither the proposals put forward in this and later chapters *nor any alternative proposals* will secure the effective working of the kind of democracy to which both the Labour Party and the Co-operative movement stand fully committed in principle, though not by the test of actual behaviour.

With these preliminaries I can now come to by far the most difficult part of my task—the formulation of plans for the democratic 'socialisation' of that part of retail trade which is at present in the hands of large-scale capitalist *entrepreneurs*. I have already explained why I want to leave the small private shopkeeper in being. But why, it may be asked, stop there? Why not recognise that, as the Co-operative movement, with its present capital resources and organisation, is clearly not in a position to take over the major part of retail trade, the big private shopkeeper and the capitalist shopkeeping company should also be left to carry on indefinitely, subject only to such controls as may be imposed on them for the prevention of monopoly practices or for the regulation of conditions of employment? As I see the matter, there are two main reasons against this. In the first place, I believe the present system of shopkeeping to be grossly wasteful of resources and to result in unnecessarily wide margins and inflated retail prices. I believe competition in quality of service to be a good thing, up to a point; but the existing forms of competition in retail trade are duplication run mad and involve not only gross waste of man-power and capital resources in the distributive processes themselves, but also failure to secure the proper advantages of mass-production of consumers' goods, through the placing of large regular orders and the elimination of varieties that are of no benefit to the final buyers. Secondly, I have a positive belief in the virtues of the 'mutual' type of trading of which the Consumers' Co-operative movement is the existing exemplar, and want to see this method extended much more widely than there seems any likelihood that it will be through the Co-operative movement as it is by the existing methods of competitive growth. As a Socialist, I am also moved by a desire to supersede large-scale capitalist enterprise, wherever possible, in favour of economic arrangements more consistent with the requirements of a society based on social equality.

THE LONG-RUN PROBLEM

To say all this is not to say that I desire to single out large-scale private trading for elimination at an early stage in the transition from Capitalism to Socialism. The proposals which I am about to put forward are to be regarded, not as ripe for immediate execution in their entirety, but rather as a basis for concerted long-term planning by the Labour Party in consultation with the Co-operative movement. Some things I should like to see done at once, or at the earliest possible opportunity; but the whole plan is meant to be spread in its execution over a considerable time. What I have in mind, in relation to the plan as a whole, is a stage in the growth of a socialised economy considerably beyond that which has been reached already—a stage at which one form or another of public ownership has already made large further advances in the fields of industrial production and the conduct of international bulk trade in essential foodstuffs and materials. I am assuming, when such a stage has been reached, a decision by the Government to eliminate large-scale capitalism from some, if not from all, branches of retail trading and to substitute some form of non-profit-seeking enterprise.

POSSIBLE WAYS OF SOCIALISATION

There are several possible ways in which this would be done. I am here thinking of chains of grocery, drapery, furnishing, hardware and similar stores, and of big department stores, rather than of more specialised undertakings. These latter would in some cases be essentially retail outlets for large manufacturing businesses, and might be more appropriately dealt with as subsidiaries of such businesses and taken over in conjunction with them. They can accordingly be considered best when we come to discuss the future of Co-operative manufacturing production. The more general chains and big department stores, on the other hand, belong essentially to the distributive sector, and I am accordingly setting out to consider how they can be dealt with *when the time comes* to convert them to forms consistent with the requirements of what the Co-operative leaders have recently called, in their manifesto of 1950, 'a collectivist economy'.

Obviously one way would be for the State to purchase the undertakings which it wished to take over, in the same way as it has bought out the gas and electricity undertakings, and then to run them under the auspices of some sort of Public Corporation, with whatever degree of regional and local autonomy might seem to be most appropriate. I think, however, that this would be a thoroughly bad way of tackling the problem, and certainly it would meet with the most determined opposition from the Co-operative movement.

The second way would be for the State, after taking over the businesses in question, to hand them over to the local government authorities to be run as municipal undertakings. There is more to be said in favour of this, at any rate in the towns, though it would give rise to considerable difficulties in the smaller areas; but I do not think that it would really work well. A municipal authority is not well equipped for carrying on a variety of retail businesses which would need to hold large and diverse stocks and to cater for individual tastes over a wide field. The local authorities would be embarrassed by finding themselves conducting businesses in competition with those belonging to some of their individual members, and the Co-operative movement would assuredly resist this solution with fully as much determination as it would direct State trading under a Public Corporation.

I do not mean, by what I have just said, to exclude all forms of municipal shopkeeping—far from it. I am strongly in favour of municipal restaurants and municipal public-houses; I should like to see large developments of municipal trade in utility furniture, furnishings and fittings as an outgrowth of municipal house-supply; I favour handing back the local management of gas and electricity distribution to local or regional bodies and the fullest provision, in connection with them, of shops for the sale or hire of gas and electrical appliances; I think there is much to be said in favour of municipal garages and petrol stations, as well as of municipal cinemas, dance halls, concert halls and theatres. I do not, however, regard the local government authority as a suitable body to carry on the general trade in consumers' goods.

A third alternative way of superseding large-scale capitalist retailing would be for the State, having bought out the businesses in question, either to sell them outright to the Co-operative movement, if it could find the capital required for buying them, or, alternatively, to lease them to the local Co-operative Stores, if necessary providing a part of the working capital needed for their conduct. The local Consumers' Co-operative Societies would then presumably amalgamate the businesses thus acquired with their existing undertakings, retaining such central emporia or branch shops as they thought fit to carry on, and closing down the rest. This would involve the customers of the establishments taken over becoming members of the local Co-operative Societies, presumably by the traditional method of accumulating share capital gradually out of accrued dividends; but as the accumulation of sufficient capital by this method would take a long time, the local Co-operative Societies would have either to apply their own reserves to the financing of their newly acquired trade or to borrow the necessary additional capital from the State, or from some other agency set up by the State for this purpose—for there seems to be no alternative source from which the money could come.

This would involve a big influx into the existing Co-operative Societies of members with no understanding of Co-operative methods and ideals, and in some cases quite out of sympathy with them. It might be practicable for the Co-operative movement in time to absorb and sufficiently to educate in Co-operative principles so large a body of involuntary recruits, but evidently this could be achieved only by an immense educational campaign spread over a considerable period of time. Indeed, this solution might involve the abandonment of any idea of making more than a small minority of Co-operative purchasers at all conscious of the social aims of Co-operation. It may be said that only a minority to-day possesses this awareness, and that the addition of a few more millions to the ten millions already enrolled would not make a great deal of difference; but I think it would, in fact, have considerable effects, unless it had been preceded by a great change in public opinion. Under present conditions, such an influx would make it much easier for short-sighted Co-operators, intent mainly on dividends and hostile to 'political' and idealistic tendencies in the movement, to pack Quarterly Meetings in opposition to sound policies of development; and the existence of this increased danger would tend to make Management Committees and managers even more cautious than they now are. In particular, the influx of a large number of new members quite uneducated in Co-operative ideas would tend to weaken the ties between Co-operation and the Labour movement. It would, for example, be likely to lead to many secessions of Co-operative Societies from the Co-operative Party and to much more opposition to collaboration with Trade Unions and local Labour Parties. It might lead to a severance of the Co-operative Union from the National Council of Labour, and to a resumption of the strictly non-political line which was officially taken by the Co-operative movement up to 1917, when the Co-operative Party was formed. These are not final objections, and they rest on the assumption that political party divisions are likely to continue in something like their present form. They may be much less formidable in twenty or thirty years' time than they appear to-day; but for the present at any rate they appear formidable enough.

'MUTUALISATION'

This brings me to the fourth, and I think the only remaining, alternative. This would be for the State, after taking over the private retail undertakings which it had decided to acquire, to convert them to some sort of 'mutual' basis rather on the lines of the suggestion put forward by the Labour Party in 1949 for the 'mutualisation' of Industrial Insurance. It might turn out that, when the time comes for the supersession of a substantial section of large-scale profit-making retail business, the Co-operative movement would be unwilling or unready, for the reasons already given, to absorb into itself so large a body of new business and of new members unfamiliar with Co-operative ideas, and that the State itself might have to undertake the earlier stages of the conversion of these sections of private business by stages to a Co-operative form. This could be done in the following way. The State could buy out the share capital of the businesses to be acquired, and could itself, through an appropriate agency, provide the working capital for the carrying on of the transferred undertakings in the form of repayable loans bearing a fixed rate of interest. At the same time, the transferred businesses could be reorganised on Co-operative lines, with opportunities for the customers to receive dividends on their purchases and to allow these dividends, or a part of them, to remain in the businesses as share capital. The loan capital provided by the State could then be paid off as fast as the members were in a position to replace it by share capital or loan stock of their own providing. The new 'mutualised' businesses would thus turn gradually into fully fledged Co-operative Societies.

But would this come about? It is most unlikely that the consumers who had been the customers of the shops transferred from profit trading to a mutual basis would wish, or be able, to invest the capital needed for their conduct, at any rate except over a long period of years. The existing capital resources of the Co-operative movement have been built up slowly over a long time, mainly out of accrued dividends which have been allowed to accumulate as small savings. Even if the fullest encouragement were given to consumers, not only to let their dividends remain in the hands of the new 'Mutuals', but also to invest in them out of past savings, it would be many years before more than a small fraction of the capital could come to be owned by the consuming members. Evidently, the new 'Mutuals' would have, at the outset, to be State-owned, and could pass only very gradually under the ownership of their members—if they ever did, in any full sense. This, of course, would not prevent them from paying dividends on purchases to their customers, as a few private traders do now; but it would differentiate them sharply from the existing Co-operative Societies, which are entirely independent of public finance.

It would mean, too, that the new 'Mutuals' would not, like the existing Consumers' Societies, be in possession of surplus resources for investment in wholesale trade or in production. The wholesale agencies supplying them would also need to be financed from public funds, even if they too were put on a 'mutual' basis in respect of their government and of the payment of dividends on purchases to the Societies they supplied.

It has, of course, to be borne in mind that quite a large proportion of the customers of the private businesses thus taken over and converted into 'mutual' agencies would be already accustomed to dealing for a part of their purchases at the 'Co-op.'. It is altogether a mistake to think of the customers of the private shops and of the Co-operative Stores as two separate sets of persons. Few Co-operators buy from their local 'Co-op' everything they need that it sets out to sell; a great many deal with it only for a few kinds of goods, a good many for only one kind—say, bread, or milk, or coal. This means that in many cases the Co-operative Societies and the proposed new 'Mutuals' would be in competition for the savings as well as for the trade of their customers. Probably, those who were prepared to invest at all would let their accumulating dividends stay with the supplier of whom they had bought the goods on which the dividend was earned; but the limits of capital accumulation in both types of retail concern would be set by the willingness and ability of the customers to save and by the rival attractions of Co-operative or 'Mutual' investment, on the one hand, and investment in Building Societies, or insurance policies, or in National Savings bonds or certificates, on the other.

Evidently, the objection to such a form of 'mutualisation', at both the retail and the wholesale levels, is that the members of the 'Mutuals', trading not with their own money but with the State's, would not have the same incentives to caution as apply to the existing Co-operative Societies, which are well aware of their responsibilities as trustees for their members' savings. Even in face of this responsibility, local Consumers' Societies do occasionally go wrong, and get into financial difficulties from which the Wholesale Societies have to rescue them, either by nursing them back to health or by taking them over and carrying them on as branches of the retail agencies they have set up for this purpose. If some of the new 'Mutuals' got into similar difficulties, they would have to turn for help to the State or to some agency set up by it; and the State, or its agency, would have to be armed with power either to assist, or to close down, or to provide for carrying on the business. Closing down would probably be the correct policy in some instances, though not in most; but this would mean that, unless the State guaranteed any part of the capital of such a body that was owned by the purchasing members, investment in a 'Mutual' would be less safe than investment in a Co-operative Society nowadays usually is. In practice, I think the State would have to guarantee the security of the members' investments, if it were desired to encourage the growth of mutual ownership.

This would mean, in effect, that, for some time at any rate, the 'Mutuals' would be trading, in the last resort, at the public risk, and not at their own. This would involve the laying down of strict rules governing the determination of the disposable surplus, which would settle how much could be distributed in dividends on purchases. The 'Mutuals' would have a strong incentive to efficiency in that the dividend would depend on the size of the surplus, after costs and fixed interest charges, including interest to the State on its capital investment, had been met. There would also have to be rules governing allocations to reserves and costs of depreciation; and there might need to be provision for the gradual amortisation of the publicly owned capital, on the lines of the clauses included in recent nationalisation Acts. I am assuming that the process of 'mutualisation' would include the buying-out by the State of the private shareholders, either in cash or by the issue of State bonds not charged against the particular enterprises taken over, but constituting part of the public debt.

RE-GROUPING THE 'MUTUALS'

It would, of course, be necessary in any such process of 'mutualisation' to reorganise the structure of the transferred undertakings, which could be re-grouped into convenient units within each suitable area. This would involve in some cases the breaking-up of existing undertakings operating in a number of places, and also some closing down of redundant businesses. If a number of capitalist trading concerns were to be 'mutualised' in this way, so as to be gradually given a Co-operative character but to be left separate from the existing Co-operative Societies, the effect would be to establish a system of *competing* Co-operative trading agencies side by side in most towns and in some villages. This would, of course, confront the Co-operative movement with a totally new situation. Although competition between Co-operative Societies in a single locality is not unknown, the policy of the Consumers' Co-operative movement has been for a long time past to eliminate overlapping, wherever possible, between rival local Societies, and to delimit trading areas so as to avoid conflicts of jurisdiction. The cases in which rival Co-operative Societies are still in competition one with another within the same areas for trade and members are exceptional, and it would be a very great departure from Co-operative tradition to recognise local competition as the normal practice. This, however, is by no means to say that the solution of turning large-scale private trading agencies into 'Mutuals' without amalgamating them with the existing Co-operative Societies is necessarily wrong. It may have been quite right for Co-operative Societies to do their utmost to eliminate overlapping as long as they have been in direct competition with large-scale private traders, but it might be highly undesirable, if large-scale private trading ceased to exist, to replace it by such an extension of the existing Co-operative movement as would result in each area in a local monopoly of large-scale distribution, even if rival small-scale trading agencies continued to exist outside the ring.

COMPETITIVE CO-OPERATION

The establishment of the Co-operative, or 'Mutual Trading', type of store as the sole form of large-scale distributive enterprise may well require, at any rate in towns of any size, the existence of more than one Co-operative Society—in the larger places of a substantial number. This would lead to a situation in which, just as many Co-operative members now spread their purchases between the local Co-operative Society and a number of private shops, the individual consumers would in many cases be trading members of several local Societies, which would be competing for their custom by offering good service. This idea of the future of Consumers' Co-operation may be novel, and unwelcome, to many Co-operative leaders; but there is surely a great deal to be said in its favour. The Co-operatives at present are kept up to scratch by the competition of other kinds of traders; a monopoly of large-scale retail trading in the hands of a single agency is hardly to be desired from the consumers' point of view. Why not have rival Co-operative Societies and 'Mutuals' in the same area to keep one another up to the mark?

The question that at once arises, if this solution is to be adopted, is that of the relations between the existing Co-operative Societies and the 'mutualised' Societies created by the transformation of large-scale capitalist trading agencies to a Co-operative form. Are the new 'Co-operatives', for example, to become members of the Co-operative Wholesale Society and of the Co-operative Union and its Sections and Districts, and thus to be integrated into the existing movement? It can be assumed that 'mutualisation' would involve the adoption of dividends on purchases and of fixed interest payments on share capital, in accordance with the 'Rochdale model', whether or not it included also the insistence on 'cash trading', subject to such modifications of that principle as many of the existing Co-operatives have been led to accept. There would be no bar, as far as mutual trading principles are concerned, in the way of the entry of the new 'Mutuals' into the Co-operative Union and the Wholesale Societies; but probably there would be no compulsory affiliation to either of these bodies, and it would be left for them to join or not as they pleased.

'MUTUAL' WHOLESALING

There would, indeed, be, as part of the change, an immediate development of 'Mutual' Wholesale Agencies side by side with the 'mutualised' retail shops; for the 'chains' taken over under the scheme would have their own wholesale departments, which would be acquired together with their retail outlets, and could be kept in being and re-grouped as 'Mutual' Wholesales serving the new retail 'Mutuals'. The retail 'Mutuals' could be given immediately a share in the control of these Wholesales and could be encouraged to invest in them as soon as they had acquired more capital than they needed for financing their local concerns. The 'Mutual' Wholesales, run at first with State funds and under managements mainly nominated to represent the public interest, could thus be gradually transformed into fully Co-operative ventures, in the same way as the retail 'Mutuals'—the pace of the transformation depending on the rate of capital accumulation through members' investments in the retail 'Mutual' Societies.

CONSUMERS' CAPITAL

As many capitalist retail businesses—especially the large chain-store concerns—cover a wide area and are not localised in the same way as the existing Co-operative Societies, it would have to be decided whether, under 'mutualisation', they were to be broken up, in respect of their retail outlets, into local units of greater or less extent, or some of them were to be left to operate on a national or regional scale. It would be difficult to apply to them any real form of consumers' control unless they were broken up into units covering areas small enough for the consumers to be able to meet together, as in the existing Co-operative Societies,[1] and to develop enough cohesion to give some meaning to elections. If, however, this breaking-up process were undertaken, there would have to go with it some amalgamation and re-grouping of the shops taken over and of the wholesale agencies connected with them; and there might well emerge from such a process a limited number of large-scale retail suppliers in each area, linked up with a still smaller number of competing wholesale agencies. The existing retail Co-operative Societies would thus take their place as one group, no doubt the largest and most

[1] Some of which already cover a wide area and hold local as well as central meetings.

influential, among a number of retail trading agencies, all resting on a Co-operative basis, but continuing in competition with small-scale private traders, and with specialist retail outlets attached to certain forms of productive business or to specialist services, such as gas and electricity, for the supply of consumers' appliances.

'BAZAAR' TRADING

In certain cases there might be powerful reasons for maintaining particular 'chains' as national concerns, operated under some form of public ownership and management. For example, such 'bazaar' trading concerns as Woolworths and the very successful multiple dress business built up by Marks and Spencer raise special problems, because their success depends essentially on the possession of large enough assured outlets for popular 'lines' to enable them to place very big orders with suppliers and in many cases to take the entire output of considerable firms. This bulk purchase makes it possible to cut costs very low and to encourage the elimination of unnecessary varieties without any real restriction of consumers' choice—for each individual shop can carry at least as large a stock of varieties as any competitor, while the total number of varieties is greatly reduced at the manufacturing end. In many classes of goods, this result can be largely achieved by reducing the number of wholesale agencies supplying the retailers, without the wholesale agency actually owning the retail outlets. But in the special cases of the Woolworth and Marks and Spencer types of trade, unified ownership of the retail outlets is probably a necessary condition of securing the full economies of long runs and standardised production.

WOULD 'MUTUALISATION' WORK?

Would such a scheme of 'mutualisation' as I have outlined in this chapter really work? The case against it is that the consumers who at present buy their goods from a wide variety of private traders show no sign of a desire to become the owners or controllers of the shops with which they deal. Indeed, they cannot be expected to show such a desire; for who wants to become part-owner or part-controller of perhaps a dozen different businesses from which he, or she, makes regular purchases? Those who do want to control the shops they buy at can get a large part of what they want by patronising the local Co-operative Society. The rest of the shoppers are not in the least likely to be excited by the prospect of 'mutualisation'—though a number of them might quite like the notion of receiving dividends on what they bought.

It is not, however, suggested that 'mutualisation' should be extended over the whole range of private trade. All that I have suggested is that it should be applied in the first instance experimentally to a limited group of large department stores and capitalist chain stores which need to be taken out of private hands but cannot easily be taken over by the existing Co-operative movement. The State, in reorganising this group of capitalist enterprises on a mutual basis, would need to re-group them. For example, in a town of 100,000 inhabitants, serving a further 50,000 or so outside its borders, all the chain-store grocers, except the Co-operative Society, could be re-grouped as branches of a single 'Mutual', linked to a common 'Mutual' Wholesale supplier. Drapers, bootmakers and other chain-store branches could be similarly grouped, so as to provide in each trade a large-scale specialist competitor with the local Co-operative Society and with the small-scale traders, who would not be interfered with. The department stores could be let alone, at any rate for the time being, where they were independent local ventures. Where they were branches of large capitalist concerns, they could be converted into local 'Mutuals' controlled, as 'Federal Societies', by the specialised local and wholesale 'Mutuals' of the various trades.

It will be observed that I am not proposing to set up, side by side with the local Co-operative Societies, a parallel system of multiple dealing, but rather to leave in rivalry with the Co-operatives several more specialised 'Mutual' concerns, each engaged mainly in a single line of business. Each of these would need to be linked up on a national (or possibly a regional) scale with a strong central buying agency, which could in course of time become federally organised, like the C.W.S., under the control of its local member 'Mutuals'. From the outset this would make it easy for the local 'Mutuals' to place mass orders and to achieve the full economies of large-scale, standardised production.

Under the conditions suggested, the consumer would be dealing at most only with a quite small number of the new 'Mutuals' —probably, at the outset, if the plan were introduced gradually, with very few. He could please himself about becoming a shareholder; if his purchases exceeded a certain sum during any period, he would automatically become entitled to attend and vote at members' meetings and take part in the election of a controlling committee. As long as the State owned a large part of the capital, it could retain the right to appoint certain members to the committee, some of them on the advice of the local government authorities in the area, or could delegate the right of appointment of some members to these authorities. The committee could appoint managers, and the employees could be given the right to elect one or more members to represent them. The committees thus constituted would in turn elect, or take part in electing, a controlling committee for the local department store, where one existed on a 'Mutual' basis; and here again certain seats could be reserved for national and local authority nominees and for the employees. This central committee could act as a co-ordinating body for the whole group of 'Mutuals', and could discuss with the local Co-operative Society any matters of common concern.

This may not be precisely the best structure. I set it down, not dogmatically, but in order to give a clear example of how matters could be arranged. There are many possible variants, and there is no reason why the structure should be the same in all places.

THE CASE FOR 'MUTUALISATION'

I do not, then, regard the probable apathy of the majority of the members to the proposed 'Mutual' trading concerns as a valid argument against 'mutualisation'. This apathy exists already in the majority of Co-operative members, and even the most hopeful forecasts of the future of Consumers' Co-operation do not go beyond the hope of increasing the size of the active minority. All that is needed to give the 'Mutuals' a reasonable chance is a large enough group of interested consumers to constitute fair-sized members' meetings and to supply the quite small numbers of 'activists' to serve on committees and to provide enough criticism to keep committees and managers up to scratch. In the early stages many of these activists would be men and women who have already some experience of activity in the Co-operative Stores. Moreover, in the 'Mutuals' the tendency should be for the housewives, rather than their husbands, to play the predominant part. The legacy of the times when women were regarded as unsuitable to take part in business operations still lies heavy on many Co-operative Societies, especially in the older industrial areas, where men still form the bulk of the membership. In the 'Mutuals', the actual shoppers would be the members; and I fancy it would not be difficult quite rapidly to build up sufficient bodies of actively interested members, with women taking the predominant place. One effect I should hope for from such a development would be an increase in the part played by women in controlling the Co-operative movement as well.

The case for 'mutualisation' rests, however, fundamentally on the need to find some way of replacing private capitalism in the field of retail trade without creating in its place a state bureaucratic trading machine. As soon as the question is, not whether private capitalism is to continue, but what is to take its place, it becomes necessary to choose between some form of 'mutualisation' and State or municipal enterprise. Of these alternatives, I regard 'mutualisation' as in general the best; but, as the State will have to provide the capital, at any rate initially, in default of any other possible source, and as a good deal of consumer apathy is probable in the early stages, it seems sensible to strengthen the managing committees with nominees of the local authorities and of the employees. The 'Mutuals' would thus differ considerably from the Co-operative Societies, with which they would be in competition. The dangers of monopoly would be avoided, and the public authorities would be relieved of the heavy administrative burdens which outright nationalisation or municipalisation would involve.

No doubt, a good many ardent Co-operators will take strong exception to these proposals, and will argue that the right course is so to transform the existing Co-operative movement as to render it capable of doing the entire job without setting up any newfangled 'Mutuals' in competition with it. But how do those who take this line expect the transformation to be brought about? There is not the smallest sign of the Co-operative leadership meaning to make itself ready to take over the bulk of retail trade, or of members of the Co-operative Societies being prepared to endorse such a policy were the leaders to recommend it. The cautious conservatism of the Co-operative movement is no mere accident of the persons who lead it lacking enterprise; it is inherent in the whole structure of the movement, with its ultimate dependence on the votes of the members who attend Quarterly Meetings—most of them mainly interested in the next quarter's dividend. No amount of propaganda will by istelf alter this situation, which can be altered only by a fundamental change in the social environment. Not until there is a large, well-organised workers' party, with a clear-cut policy based on Socialist conceptions, equipped to send its missionaries into every Co-operative Society as well as into every Trade Union, not merely to conduct propaganda but to undertake the constructive work of control and management in accordance with a concerted plan, can the Co-operative movement be roused out of its conservative slumber. But even such a body of missionaries could not hope, within any measurable time, to turn the Co-operative Societies into bodies capable of taking over and running successfully the bulk of retail trade in all its branches. They would have much better hope of success if they could work simultaneously in the Co-operatives and in the other sections of retail trade, using the 'Mutuals' as means of stirring up the Co-operative Societies, and also of enlisting a larger body of active and conscious consumers to take an interest in the efficiency of the agencies supplying them with the everyday means of life.

AN INTERIM PROPOSAL

I have already explained that these proposals for the 'mutualisation' of retail trade are not put forward for immediate, or even for early, adoption in full. There are, however, certain advances towards them that could be made at once. As long as the State takes action to maintain full employment and therewith a high level of consumers' demand, the more efficient or well-placed private trading agencies will be bound to make high profits with very little risk. Why should not all joint stock concerns engaged in retail trade be compelled by law to pay 'dividends on purchases' to their customers in the same way as Co-operative Societies? It might be necessary to exclude merely casual purchasers, as happens now in the case of the Co-operatives and of private traders who have adopted the 'dividend'. But every regular customer could be entitled to a dividend, which would have to be assessed in accordance with the trading profits. This would of course involve some limitation of the dividends on capital paid to the shareholders, and some definition of the conditions governing the allocation of profits to reserve. But it would not be at all difficult to work out a satisfactory system—to some extent on the lines of the legal regulation of gas dividends and selling prices before gas was taken over as a public service.

FACING THE FUTURE

I am fully aware that much of what has been said in this chapter will be regarded by many of my readers as rather absurd, and will be brushed aside by many as a foolish attempt at crossing bridges before they are reached. But, if what I have suggested is to be rejected, what alternatives have either Socialists or believers in the 'Co-operative Commonwealth' in mind? They cannot really intend large-scale capitalist distributive business to go on as it is for ever; and they must have, at the least, some hazy idea in their minds of what they intend to do about it when the time comes. They may prefer, on tactical grounds, to evade public discussion of such non-immediate issues; but they will not be able to arrive at any clear agreement about the kind of society they are aiming at unless they are prepared to go some way towards facing such problems, at any rate in their own minds.

THE PROSPECT FOR RETAIL TRADE

Thus, for some time to come it seems likely that retail trade will remain organised much as it is at present, with a large, but by no means dominant, Co-operative sector in direct competition with the various types of private agency. The Co-operatives seem unlikely, without drastic changes of method, to encroach very rapidly on the private sector, even in those branches of trade in which they are most securely entrenched. Nor do they seem likely, in venturing upon new types of retailing, to be in a position to expand very fast, or to make their adventures on a scale large enough to alter appreciably the general trading structure. They have neither capital enough nor the organisation for a really great challenge to the private traders; and even if the State were prepared to advance capital to them on favourable terms for the expansion of their operations it seems likely that they would hesitate to accept any such offer, for fear of increasing fixed interest obligations in connection with capital projects a good deal riskier than they are accustomed to—to say nothing of the danger of swamping their existing membership with a large accession of new members entirely unaccustomed to Co-operative methods and principles. That is why it has seemed necessary to suggest the alternative of 'mutualisation' which I have put forward in this chapter; but I fully accept the fact that the time cannot be ripe for the full developments that I have outlined until the way towards them has been opened up both by a further growth of Socialist opinion among the electorate and by a great advance in the practical vision and ambitions of Co-operators themselves.

Accordingly, for the present the problems of reducing waste of man-power in the retail distributive trades, and of securing a fair deal for the consumer in terms of price and quality, will have to be tackled mainly by forms of control which will keep down distributive margins, and thus make it less easy to open redundant shops, and will also disallow undesirable forms of monopolistic trade association and price-maintenance agreements of a restrictive tendency. The competitive position of the Co-operative Societies could at this stage be strengthened by forbidding discrimination against them by manufacturers of branded goods and by removing all restrictions that prevent payment of dividends on purchases of such goods as are offered for sale at standard prices fixed by the manufacturer or wholesale supplier. But discussion of such questions as these would take me well outside the limited scope and purpose of this book.

Chapter VI

THE CASE OF INDUSTRIAL INSURANCE

*

THE solution suggested in the previous chapter is to some extent analogous to that which the Labour Party, in November 1949, decided to adopt in the disputed case of the insurance industry. Originally the Labour Party, following the recommendation of the Beveridge Report, intended to nationalise industrial insurance (and other branches of insurance closely connected with it) by taking over the existing concerns, including the Co-operative Insurance Society, and fusing them into a single agency under public ownership. In face of Co-operative and other protests, this intention was revised, and it was decided instead to convert the insurance *companies* affected into mutual societies, similar to those which already carry on a substantial section of the business, but at the same time to bring all the agencies concerned under the control of a central public body, with sufficient powers to bring about amalgamations, to reduce overlapping and waste of man-power, and to exercise some control over the investment of the large funds which the insurance agencies administer as trustees for their policy-holders. Such arrangements would seem to present considerable advantages, provided that the central co-ordinating power is strong enough to achieve the large economies that are possible only if duplication can be greatly reduced. After all, a mutual insurance society is a kind of Co-operative Society, wherever it lives up to its principles by allowing its policy-holders a real control over its affairs. In many countries where such mutual bodies exist they are called Co-operative Societies, and are recognised as parts of the Co-operative movement. In Great Britain we are accustomed to use the word 'Co-operative' in a narrower sense; but this does not alter the fact that *mutual* insurance societies are essentially Co-operative in form, if not in actual working, so that, if their Co-operative character can be made a reality, there is scope in them for a big extension of the province of Co-operative enterprise.

The difficulty lies, of course, in the enormous number of the policy-holders, and in the scant interest most of them take in the societies, even when these are formally organised on a mutual basis. This applies much less to the Friendly Society Orders with local branches than to the huge Collecting Societies without branches, over which the nominal members exercise practically no real control. It applies in varying degrees to the numerous smaller local societies, in some of which the members participate actively, whereas others have only the barest forms of democratic control. If such *companies* as the Prudential and the Pearl are now to be converted to a mutual basis, it will be necessary to attempt to endow them with a real local life, and to make the same attempt in the case of the *societies* which are at present run only nominally on a mutual basis. This will not be possible in either case if each insurance office is to continue to be treated as an entirely separate unit; for in the normal running of the business of industrial insurance there is certainly not enough to interest the main body of the policy-holders in each office to carry on an effective local organisation—a great deal less than there is to interest the ordinary Co-operator in the running of his retail store.

It is, indeed, almost inconceivable that any attempt to breathe effective life into local branches consisting of the policy-holders of a particular collecting society (or mutualised big company) could succeed. There would be a much better prospect of success if in each area a single body were to be set up, including all the policy-holders irrespective of the society to which they belonged, to act as a collective local vigilance organisation for dealing with complaints and problems in relation to the local operations of any society operating in the area. The areas for such bodies would need to be small, and based either on residence or, in the case of large factories, possibly on the place of work. Each of them would elect a local committee, which could easily take on additional functions—for example, that of dealing with local complaints and problems arising out of the administration of the

National Insurance and Public Health services as well as with industrial insurance. They could even take on, in some places, the functions of Citizens' Advice Bureaux, either on their own account or in conjunction with other agencies already in the field.

The creation of such local bodies, not limited to members of a particular society, would greatly aid the process of amalgamation and squeezing out of redundant and duplicating services. The local committees could have direct access to the central co-ordinating body which it is proposed to set up to supervise the separate societies, and their activities would make policy-holders much more conscious than they now are of the widely varying advantages offered by competing societies, and would thus promote greater uniformity of provision, to the extent to which uniformity is desirable in the interest of the policy-holders as a means to improved services.

Immediately, this seems to be the only possible way of making mutualisation really work, so as to secure some measure of effective consumers' influence. There is, however, another way in which, in the longer run, industrial insurance might be organised on far more democratic lines. Already, in a good number of countries, Co-operative insurance is strongly established on a foundation quite different not only from that of the British companies and nominally mutual societies, but also from that of the Co-operative Insurance Society owned and controlled by the British C.W.S. This method is that of the small mutual society, called in some countries a Co-operative Bank and in the United States a 'Credit Union', set up usually by a body of fellow-employees in a particular establishment or service, or by a group of small farmers or shopkeepers. These bodies, which have behind them a history of more than a century, are primarily agencies for the investment of small savings and the making of small loans to meet their members' needs. They have developed very rapidly in the United States during the past twenty years, and form a major element in the American Co-operative movement of to-day. Designed primarily as savings and loans agencies, they can readily take on, through federal bodies of their own, long-term insurance and endowment policies, and can conduct their business with very much lower overhead expenses than bodies which depend on salaried house-to-house collecting agents.

In Great Britain, this type of mutual thrift agency has never so far made much headway, though of course Great Britain has its Trustee Savings Banks, with a long history behind them. It has failed to catch on mainly because of the keen competition of the great insurance concerns on the doorsteps of the potential customers, and also because of the unhappy experience of a large number of proprietary thrift agencies started by promoters, sometimes fraudulent, for their own profit. Something rather like it, but not on a Co-operative basis, has grown up in recent years in the Savings Groups promoted under the auspices of the National Savings movement; and there seems to be no valid reason why these should not serve as the nucleus for a much bigger development, or why they should not be re-cast on more fully Co-operative lines. This, however, would take time; and in the interim the mutualisation of the insurance business, on the grouped basis that I have suggested, would be a step in the right direction. The local committees of the mutualised service could set to work to create small mutual societies of the type that have been so successful elsewhere; and in course of time the entire structure of insurance might be transformed and endowed with a really democratic character.

The establishment of such a network of consumers' agencies in the field of mutual insurance would be, in effect, the addition of a new province to the Co-operative movement, which could proceed in each district to develop relations with its new auxiliary. The details of the Labour Party's revised plan were published early in 1950 in a pamphlet, *The Future of Industrial Assurance*, which replaced the nationalisation scheme embodied in *Labour Believes in Britain.* Categorical assurances were given that under the scheme of 'mutualisation', the reformed offices would be left full freedom to conduct their business in the interests of the policy-holders. The existing shareholders were to be bought out on fair terms of compensation, and compensation was also to be paid to agents in respect of what is called 'book interest'. This arises out of the anomalous situation which exists in a number of concerns whereby the insurance agent has a right to nominate his successor by selling to him for a capital sum the right to take over the collection of premiums and to receive the commission paid on the sums collected. The Labour Party, following the recommendations of a sequence of public committees which have studied the problem, proposed to bring this system of 'book interest' to an end, but to compensate agents who have bought their 'books'. The Party also promised that there should be no dismissals of agents, at any rate without adequate compensation, and that the reduction of staffs expected to result from improved organisation should be brought about by slowing down the recruitment of new agents.

This scheme was satisfactory up to a point, but there was in it nothing to ensure that the policy-holders, who were to become the nominal owners of the mutualised concerns, should have any effective control over their working. The policy-holders have, in practice, no real control over the existing bodies which are in the form of Collecting Societies, though these are nominally under mutual ownership. It is, indeed, impracticable to give the policy-holders any real control over a large number of separate Societies, many of which operate over the whole country, or a large part of it, without any branch organisation such as exists in the Friendly Societies proper—Oddfellows, Druids, and other recognised 'Orders'. Thus, mutualisation on the terms proposed would not of itself achieve any reality of democratic control, even though it might result in better terms for policy-holders through a reduction of the proportion of premiums absorbed in management expenses. This proportion is at present much too high, and is indeed even higher in the offices which are already in form on a mutual basis than in the profit-making companies such as the Prudential. This peculiar state of affairs is usually explained by the fact that the average sum insured is lower in the 'Mutual' Societies than in the companies, whereas the cost of collecting premiums is as great for smaller as for larger amounts. This may be true; but the facts do not hold out any prospect that mutualisation by itself will diminish the extravagant sums expended on weekly collections of small premiums.

The plain truth is that the rates of expenses can be substantially reduced only by diminishing the number of rival offices and concentrating the collection of premiums in fewer hands; or, more considerably, in the long run by decentralising the whole business into the hands of small 'Mutual' Societies of the type suggested a few pages back. This requires either an amalgamation of offices into a much smaller number, or, if this is regarded as difficult to achieve rapidly, the appointment of collectors to receive premiums in limited areas on behalf of a number of offices instead of only one. Similarly, it is impracticable to establish any real democratic control as long as in any area there are a large number of separate groups of policy-holders, each attached to a particular office, in such a way that the establishment of any sort of local control would involve the establishment of dozens of different branches in each place. If real mutualisation, with real democratic control, is to be aimed at, there is only one way of bringing it about—by setting up, in each small area, a single policy-holders' organisation open to holders of policies in *all* the offices operating in the area. Such inter-office branches could exercise control over the local agents, who would similarly operate on behalf of all the offices on whose behalf premiums were being collected locally. Such a system would leave each national office to provide such kinds of policy as its directors or managers might think fit, and would thus ensure variety and competition in the policy-holders' interests. At the same time it would convert the agents from servants of the several offices into servants of the local policy-holders' organisations, and would ensure that the agents would act as representatives of their immediate clients rather than of the separate national offices.

Under such a system, the immense number of separate offices, national and local, could be reduced so as to leave only as many as are needed in order to secure effective competition and a sufficient variety of types of policy. Costs could be substantially cut by progressive reduction of the number of agents and by the elimination of overlapping, and the requirement that investment of funds should conform to the policy-holders' interests could be squared with the need to ensure that it should also take place in accordance with the requirements of national economic policy.

These suggestions go a long way beyond what is proposed in the Labour Party's pamphlet, though also much less far than it is desirable to go in the long run. They rest on the opinion that 'mutualisation' can mean nothing unless it carries with it a real element of democratic control by the policy-holders, that such control is impracticable unless the policy-holders can be organised into real local groups, and that no such organisation can be made a reality as long as it is based on keeping separate the holders of policies in each individual office, or on continuing the system under which each agent serves a particular office rather than the policy-holders.

If this proposal were adopted, the Co-operative Insurance Society would remain in existence for the time being as a distinct body, free to operate any system of policies it pleased and to undertake collective as well as individual insurance. In many cases, Consumers' Co-operative Societies offer their members certain insurance benefits which are covered by collective premiums paid by the Societies to the C.I.S. This system could continue unchanged; the difference in respect of the C.I.S. would be that it would cease to employ its own separate agents and would compete with other offices in offering individual policies that would be handled by agents who would be handling business on behalf of a number of offices instead of one only. I can see no reason why Co-operators should object to this change if, as seems clearly the case, it is the only effective way of even beginning to put the system of industrial assurance as a whole under real democratic control.

Chapter VII

WHOLESALING—THE FOOD TRADES

*

THE WHOLESALE TRADES IN GENERAL

THE effective handling of the problem discussed in Chapter V obviously depends on what is done in the sphere of wholesale trade. At present, the wholesale trade in essential foods is largely in the hands of the Ministry of Food, under temporary powers assumed during the war; and the Ministry in the main uses the capitalist wholesale firms as its agents in dealing with the retailers, and also acts through such statutory agencies as the Wheat Commission and the Agricultural Marketing Boards. The Ministry of Food, as the sole importer of many essential foodstuffs, and the Ministry of Agriculture, as the negotiator of guaranteed farm prices with the home agricultural interests, in conjunction with the Treasury as the source of food subsidies, are in a position of effective control over the prices charged to the consumers for staple food commodities. In the non-food trades, the position differs from commodity to commodity; but the Board of Trade, despite Mr. Harold Wilson's repeated 'bonfires' of controls, has still a considerable influence over the prices of essential goods, at any rate in the 'utility' ranges. In relation to these forms of State control, the Co-operative Wholesale Societies in effect count simply as two among the many wholesale firms and agencies with which the Government departments deal, and are accorded no special privileges.

THE WHOLESALE FOOD TRADES—MEAT

Let us consider, in the first place, the branches of wholesale distribution that are under the control of the Ministry of Food. In these trades, although large economies in the actual handling and transport of supplies have been achieved by co-ordination and zoning under war conditions, the retention of the pre-war businesses as agents has prevented any thorough reorganisation, and still keeps wholesale margins in many trades at an unnecessarily high level. In the special case of the distribution of meat war-time experience points strongly to the desirability—the more so because supplies are certain to be short for many years to come—of making permanent the public organisation of the entire trade through publicly owned *abattoirs* and distributing centres dealing directly with the retailers and entirely cutting out the private wholesaler. This would involve the establishment of some sort of National Meat Board or Commission to act under the general control of the Ministry of Food, in much the same way as the National Coal Board acts under the Ministry of Fuel and Power. Such a Board could issue licences to retailers (including Co-operative Societies) who grow their own meat to continue in business under proper sanitary regulations, and it might be so constituted as to include as part-time members a minority representing producers and retail distributors (again including the Co-operative Societies under both heads). Under such an arrangement, the Co-operative Wholesale Societies would lose such functions as they at present undertake as main wholesalers of meat, but the local Co-operative Societies would retain their meat business and be free to develop it. The Board would presumably take over from the Ministry of Food the conduct of the trade in imported meat, but because of the currency and balance of payments aspects of overseas purchases and bulk supply contracts, these matters would have to remain under the final control of the Government as a whole.

The Labour Party, in its 1949 Manifesto, *Labour Believes in Britain*, declared in favour of the permanent nationalisation of the wholesale trade in meat, by making permanent the functions of the Ministry of Food as purchaser and wholesaler of both imported and home-grown supplies, up to the point of distribution to the retail butchers. It also declared in favour of the socialisation of all slaughter-houses, with a view to their development 'under municipal or other public ownership', in the interest of public health; and it advocated that such large-scale cold stores as are not already owned by the Ministry of Food should be placed under public ownership, without saying more precisely how they were to be administered. The Co-operative leadership, in its statement of policy issued in 1950 under the title of *The Co-operative Movement in a Collectivist Economy*, made no precise pronouncement on the future of the trade in meat, but categorically demanded that before any detailed decisions were made about it there should be 'full consultation with the Co-operative movement', and that the Labour Party should issue no further statement of policy on the matter without such consultation. In this field of trade, the Co-operators are indeed in something of a dilemma. They do not want to go back to the pre-war system of private wholesaling, largely in the hands of big capitalist concerns; but they are also reluctant to see the whole business handed over permanently to a State monopoly which would eliminate them from the wholesale, though not of course from the retail, trade in meat. They would prefer some sort of Co-operative system, under consumers' control, if such a system could be devised; and in such a system they would like, if possible, to retain an effective place for their own movement.

MEAT IMPORTS

Three separate, though connected, questions are here involved—the purchase and handling of both imported and home-grown meat; the ownership and management of slaughter-houses, which involve considerations of public health as well as of economics; and the ownership and management of cold stores, which raise considerations of defence as well as of normal business. For a long time to come, and probably for good and all, the importation of meat will have to be controlled by the Government; for even if difficulties about the balance of payments could be overcome, the desirability would remain of long-term agreements and bulk-purchase arrangements, especially with empire suppliers. It would, however, be fully practicable to handle meat imports through a Board or Commission on which the Co-operative movement could be given a substantial representation, provided that, as in the case of the Boards entrusted with the management of the nationalised industries, the Government—in this instance, through the Minister of Food—were given power to issue policy directions to the Commission and that the Commission's activities were brought under parliamentary control to the same extent as other nationalised industries and services. Moreover, the Commission could be empowered to delegate such of its functions as it thought fit to approved non-profit-making agencies. This would make it possible to authorise, to any extent which the Government felt to be desirable, the continuance of the Wholesale Societies as its agents in dealing with any particular branch of the trade—e.g. in arranging for purchases of meat from overseas Co-operative bodies in New Zealand, Ireland, Denmark, and other areas which possess strong Co-operative organisations of their own.

HOME-PRODUCED MEAT

The handling of home-produced meat is closely tied up with the wider relations between the Government and the farmers. As long as home agriculture is being to any extent subsidised, either by money grants or by a system of guaranteed prices, it seems clear that there must be Government purchase of supplies. This too could be handled by the proposed Commission; but it would be possible in this case to allow direct dealings under regulation between the local Consumers' Co-operative Societies, or the Wholesale Societies, and the producers, including Agricultural Co-operative bodies as well as private farmers. Consumers' Societies, including the Wholesales, could also continue to conduct their own farms, and to supply their members direct with produce raised on them, if they so desired.

SLAUGHTER-HOUSES

Slaughter-houses in the larger towns could probably be best run under municipal auspices; at any rate, under a reformed system of Local Government that would bring local-authority areas into better conformity with areas of local distribution. Indeed, a reformed local-government system might make it practicable to bring all slaughter-houses under Local or Regional Authorities, in rural as well as in urban areas. Co-operative

Societies, under such a system, would hardly demand to retain their own separate slaughter-houses, where their requirements could be more economically met by hiring space in the public slaughter-houses. But if any particular Co-operative body could put up a strong enough case for keeping its own separate establishment, there would be no difficulty in allowing this to be done, subject of course to the observance of all necessary conditions in respect of public health.

COLD STORAGE

Cold storage is so largely a matter of defence needs, as well as of economic considerations, that it seems clear that a high proportion of the plant required will have to remain under public operation. But here again there could be no objection to a licensing system that would allow Co-operative bodies to maintain their own cold stores where they wished to be at the expense in their members' interests. Cold-storage plants would need, for the most part, to be centrally rather than locally owned and operated, because of their importance for the maintenance of reserve supplies, and of their close connection with the handling of meat acquired under national bulk-purchase schemes. They could either be placed under the management of the National Meat Commission or entrusted to an *ad hoc* body closely connected with it and providing in the same way for adequate Co-operative representation.

In connection with such representation in all branches of meat trading, it is of course necessary to take account of the claims of Agricultural as well as of Consumers' Co-operative Societies. But this aspect can be better discussed when we come to consider the Agricultural Co-operative movement's place in the marketing of food products from a wider point of view.

MILK DISTRIBUTION

The case of milk presents much more complex difficulties, heavily involving the Co-operative movement. In *Labour Believes in Britain* nothing specific was said about the question. The Labour Party promised, in general terms, encouragement to

Producer Co-operatives in agriculture 'by the advance of money and in other ways'; but this promise was not directly related to milk production. The Co-operative manifesto also was silent on this issue, except for a general claim that the Labour Party should adopt no policy in respect of 'Government purchasing for the consuming public' without full prior consultation with the Co-operative movement. The strong opposition of Co-operators to the pre-war system of 'producer control' through the Milk Marketing Board is, however, well known; and although the Board has become since 1939 virtually no more than a purchasing agency controlled by the Ministry of Food, Co-operators are by no means fully satisfied with it, or prepared to resign permanently all claim to some form of consumers' control. The Williams Committee of 1948 has proposed the establishment of a National Milk Commission to control the entire handling of milk from farmer to retailer, using at the outset mainly the existing distributive and transport agencies, but with power to buy out redundant firms, to set up new depots or processing factories under its own control, and to enter the field of retailing in special cases—for example, in the new towns. Clearly, such a Commission *might*, in course of time, take over a large sector of the processing and distributing services, if it were so minded and were supported by a Government favouring such a policy. But it might equally well, with a different composition or under orders from a different kind of Government, leave the entire trade, or nearly all of it, in the existing hands, or even discriminate against the Co-operative Societies, which already control nearly a third of the total. Two members of the Williams Committee put forward a much more drastic proposal. They favoured, at some future date, though not at once, complete public ownership of both wholesale and retail milk distribution, and also of processing and transport, in order to secure the economies that could be expected to result from a fully unified service.

This more ambitious proposal, which has much to recommend it on purely technical grounds, would deprive the Co-operative Societies of one of their most successful branches of trade—unless, indeed, it were left open for the proposed Commission to accept the local Co-operators, wherever they were in a position to undertake the task, as its *sole* retail distributive agents. Even so, the Co-operative movement would be called on to hand over its numerous processing plants and wholesale depots, and might regard even the acquisition of a monopoly of the retail milk trade as inadequate compensation for the loss of its rights to provide a direct service from its own farms to the consumers. If, however, the Co-operators were allowed to continue and develop their service side by side with the service of the Commission, which would replace all other supplying agencies, a large part of the expected economies of unification would be lost.

In face of the certainty of strong Co-operative opposition, the nationalisation of the entire milk trade is unlikely to be pursued in the near future. But a return to the pre-war position is also unlikely. Up to the war, the control of milk supply and prices rested with a statutory Milk Marketing Board representing only the producers, in negotiation with a non-statutory body representing only the distributors. The final consumer was unrepresented; and the two bodies which shared the effective control both preferred high prices and limited supplies to any attempt to expand sales of liquid milk by bringing down the price. This policy involved the disposal of 'surplus' milk at much lower prices either to processors who made it into cheese or butter or to public bodies distributing free or cheap milk for babies and school-children, or under other special schemes. It also involved State subsidies for milk sold outside the regular market for liquid supplies. Since 1939, consumption of liquid milk has increased greatly, and there has been no regular 'surplus' to be disposed of at cut prices. It has come to be recognised as necessary on grounds of public health both to stimulate liquid consumption and to ensure purity and good quality by effective public control. A return to the pre-war system can be ruled out. For the time being, the Ministry of Food may continue to control the trade, using the Milk Marketing Board's machinery, but in effect leaving the Board with little power; but some time a new organisation will have to be devised, and this will probably need to take the form of a National Milk Commission responsible for price policy, supplies, and the observance of proper standards, empowered to take over and carry on any form of processing, transport, and distribution, but in practice leaving the existing local Co-operative structure intact and with room to develop, and perhaps, in suitable areas, constituting the Co-operative Societies sole retail distributors. Such a solution would not be wholly satisfactory, but it would have the advantage of subjecting the alternative forms of non-profit trading—as well as such forms of profit trading as were allowed to continue—to the test of comparative efficiency under regulations designed to ensure proper hygienic standards and to eliminate restrictive practices where they were found to exist.

AGRICULTURAL MARKETING—THE LUCAS REPORT

Over the wider field of agricultural marketing as a whole, the Lucas Committee of 1948 proposed the setting up of a series of Commodity Commissions, appointed by the Government, to replace the Ministry of Food as owners on behalf of the public of the supplies bought under guaranteed-price schemes or imported from abroad. The Commissions, it was proposed, should retain supervisory powers over the subsequent distributive processes, including the power to license distributors and to regulate their proceedings, and should also be empowered to set up their own distributing agencies in order to provide a check on the costs of other distributing concerns. These proposals were not worked out in detail, and they have not so far been acted on. The Government has, however, introduced legislation providing that, should the Agricultural Marketing Boards resume any of their pre-war functions, they should be reconstituted to include representatives of the public nominated by the Ministry of Agriculture, and should be subject to some policy control by the Minister, whose interference would, however, require the approval of a committee of investigation set up after the event. This seems an inadequate and cumbersome proposal; it would surely be preferable, broadly on the lines of the Lucas Report, to set up public controlling bodies predominantly representative of public interests and to allow the Marketing Boards representing the producers to act only subject to decisions arrived at after consultation by the supervising Commissions, on which the Co-operative movement should be strongly represented.

FRUIT AND VEGETABLES—SUGAR

In respect of agricultural marketing in general, *Labour Believes in Britain* had not much to say. In addition to the paragraphs dealing with meat wholesaling and cold storage, there were only sections dealing with fruit and vegetables, and with sugar. The first of these promised that Labour would 'take steps to improve the methods of distribution between the horticultural grower and the greengrocer's shop'. It added that 'wholesale markets for fruit and vegetables as well as for other foodstuffs will, where necessary, be re-sited, re-developed and modernised, under municipal or other public ownership'. More modern *retail* fruit and vegetable markets would also be provided; and there would be increased storage, so that more produce might be stored in time of glut for release when supplies were short. The section dealing with sugar promised the nationalisation of the British Sugar Corporation, which has a monopoly of beet-sugar manufacture, and also of all sugar manufacturing and refining concerns.

The Co-operative movement is, of course, largely interested in both these branches of trade. Most of the local Consumers' Societies sell greengroceries, though these do not form a large proportion of total Co-operative trade. The Co-operative manifesto makes no reference to the Labour Party's proposals under this head, and can presumably be taken as raising no objection, as there is nothing in the proposals, except the development of better retail markets under public ownership, that could in any way interfere with Co-operative trade, and it would presumably be open for Co-operative Societies, both consumers' and agricultural, to rent stalls in such markets where they so desired.

CO-OPERATIVE MARKETING OF FRUIT AND VEGETABLES

It seems evident that in the marketing of fruit and vegetables a much larger place needs to be taken by the Agricultural Co-operative Societies. Even if the Consumers' Societies considerably extend their trade in greengroceries—as they clearly should—this, so far from removing the need for more efficient marketing by the producers, will make it still more desirable. It ought to be possible, with the assistance of the State and with the friendly collaboration of the Consumers' Societies, to develop on a greatly expanded scale Agricultural Co-operative Societies for the grading and marketing of fruit and vegetables of many kinds. The Agricultural Societies should be able to sell both directly through market stalls and to the Consumers' Societies, under conditions which would facilitate flexible pricing for the disposal of seasonal surpluses, as well as regular arrangements for the bulk purchase of normal supplies of guaranteed quality. Grading and packing stations could be maintained at convenient points either by the Agricultural Marketing Societies or as joint ventures with the local Consumers' Co-operatives and with the 'Mutuals' proposed in an earlier chapter. The Agricultural Societies would be in a better position, aided by such assured markets as the Consumers' Societies could provide, to press improvements of quality and grading upon their members, and large economies could be achieved in marketing costs by common action between the Agricultural and the Consumers' movements.

SUGAR

The proposals relating to sugar are another matter; for the Co-operative movement is a large shareholder in the leading private concern in the trade, and would thus be considerably affected by its transfer to public ownership. Accordingly, the Co-operative manifesto makes a specific demand for full consultation before any detailed decisions are taken about the nationalisation of either beet-sugar manufacture or sugar refining. No indication is given of what the Co-operative leaders would wish to see done about the private monopolies which at present dominate these trades; it can be conjectured that they may have in mind some form of 'mutualisation' that, while taking them out of private hands, would allow the Co-operative movement to retain its position as a shareholder. There seems to be no good reason why this proposal should not be complied with, if it is made. A system of joint ownership and control by the State and the Co-operative movement, including the Agricultural as well as the Consumers' Societies, would be a very interesting experiment in a new kind of public ownership and in a new relation between the Co-operative movement and the State. The Co-operative Societies, as we have seen, already hold about thirteen million consumers' registrations for sugar, and have thus a very large interest in the trade. They are also very considerable producers, through the Wholesale Societies, of preserves and of sugar confectionery; and it is entirely legitimate for them to claim that sugar manufacture is among the trades in which they have the strongest title to be recognised as suitable agents for putting the policy of public ownership into effect, or at least as suitable participants in any public agency that may be established.

CO-OPERATIVE FARMING

It has to be borne in mind that the Co-operative movement is itself engaged in farming on a considerable scale. In 1948 the retail Consumers' Co-operative Societies owned and farmed 35,000 acres of land, and rented or leased a further 3,700 acres. The two Wholesale Societies owned and farmed nearly 28,000 additional acres. This farming land involved a capital investment of over £2 millions in land and buildings, and over £1,500,000 in stock and implements. Farm output of local Societies was valued at over £1 million, and that of the two Wholesales at over £750,000. Only about 75 local Societies, out of more than 1,000, were engaged in farming, and not all these found it profitable. But after deducting interest and depreciation charges, the local Societies as a whole had a net surplus of £26,000 (1948), and the two Wholesales a surplus of £184,000 (1947).

These figures do not include the farmers' Co-operative Societies, which in England alone had in 1948 a turnover of £12 millions by marketing their members' produce and of nearly £24 millions in respect of the purchase for members of farm requirements. These particulars cover 217 Societies. The largest items on the marketing side were eggs and poultry (£8 millions), meat, bacon and livestock (£1·5 millions), and fruit and vegetables (£3 millions). Dairy produce was only £900,000—as the Milk Marketing Board here acts as the main marketing agency. These Agricultural Societies had a paid-up share capital of about £2,500,000, and loan capital, together with the capital of the similar Societies in Wales and Scotland, brought up the total capital to well over £5 millions. This figure is of course not comparable with the figures for farming by Consumers' Societies, as it includes only the capital used in marketing or in purchasing of requisites, and excludes the capital invested in the farms themselves.

These figures represent only a tiny proportion of total agricultural output. Agricultural Co-operation in Great Britain is still very weak in comparison with its position in many other countries; and the Consumers' Societies have engaged in farming only on a small scale. Their 67,000 acres are less than one-third of one per cent. of the total land under crops and permanent grass in Great Britain; and their total marketing turnover of less than £2 millions hardly counts in the aggregate of British agricultural production. Nevertheless, the consumers' movement sets store by its farming activities, and would not readily give them up; and the agricultural societies, now organised in a separate Agricultural Co-operative Association, have made a notable recovery from the low level to which they had fallen before 1939, and can be expected to increase their scale of operations in both marketing and purchase of farm requirements.

There is still, however, only a tenuous connection between the Agricultural Co-operative Societies and the main body of the Co-operative movement. The Co-operative Wholesale Society, through its Agricultural Department, conducts a substantial trade in wheat offals, converted into feeding-stuffs, and in other agricultural requisites with the agricultural purchasing societies; but the marketing societies are unrelated to the local Consumers' Co-operatives, though one would have supposed that mutually beneficial relations could easily be built up. One reason for the failure to do this is the relative weakness of the Consumers' Societies in the fruit and vegetable trades. As we saw (p. 39), less than one in three local Co-operative Societies had in 1946 a separate shop, or shops, for the sale of greengrocery. The activity in the sale of dairy products is very much greater; but in this field some Consumers' Societies have their own farms, and in the case of milk the concentration of primary wholesaling functions in the hands of the Milk Marketing Board has fundamentally affected the position.

It will be seen from the accompanying Table that the Agricultural Marketing Societies in England had in 1948 a high concentration upon eggs and poultry, which accounted for nearly £7 millions out of their total turnover of £12 millions. Fruit and vegetables came second, with a turnover of nearly £2,700,000, and bacon third, with £1,353,000. To these figures must be added the marketing done through Agricultural Societies mainly concerned with purchases of requisites. These had a turnover of nearly £2 millions in eggs and poultry, and of £422,000 in fruit and vegetables. The combined totals are very small in relation to the volume of trade in these commodities.

The plain truth is that there has never been any effective drive towards Agricultural Co-operation in England, though it has gone somewhat farther in Wales, where small farms predominate, and in parts of Scotland. Nor has there been any real endeavour on the part of the Co-operative Union to push Agricultural Co-operation. The Co-operative Union has always been dominated exclusively by the Consumers' Societies, and has tended to regard Co-operation among farmers as only a form of profit-making, to be disregarded in forming national policy just as much as the industrial Producers' Societies, if not even more. Similarly, the Co-operative Wholesale Society, though ready enough to get the custom of the Agricultural Requirements Societies for the by-products of its flour mills, has never been interested in the development of Agricultural Co-operation as an independent branch of the movement. The long-drawn-out struggle in Ireland between the C.W.S., with its own chain of creameries, and the Irish Agricultural Organisation Society, led by Sir Horace Plunkett, undoubtedly affected the outlook both of the C.W.S. and of the local Consumers' Societies to which

TABLE

AGRICULTURAL CO-OPERATIVE SOCIETIES—

	No. of Societies	*Members*	*Paid-up Shares, £s*	*Reserves*	*Loans and Overdraft*	*Sales of Reqirements*
A. REQUIREMENTS:						
up to £20,000	23	2,805	9,079	19,246	2,139	119,894
£20–50,000 .	9	1,915	32,159	23,045	5,527	285,243
£50–100,000 .	15	8,719	98,504	102,951	50,836	964,734
£100–250,000 .	17	10,993	223,591	314,280	24,319	2,678,549
£250–500,000	10	13,937	399,226	303,105	145,234	3,335,536
£500,000+ .	5	19,435	534,196	400,494	415,946	5,282,038
Multi-purpose .	8	18,814	533,900	521,944	311,015	4,820,771
GRAND TOTAL (A)	87	76,618	—	—	—	—
B. MARKETING:						
Dairy . .	7	886	74,700	49,708	42,029	—
Eggs and Poultry . .	20	24,371	184,384	105,838	22,206	15,005
Livestock Auctions .	3	469	6,554	5,778	402	—
Bacon . .	3	4,417	86,652	119,691	5,915	—
Wool . .	4	3,723	12,691	13,715	—	—
Fruit and Vegetables .	15	5,044	146,020	103,045	99,456	180,527
Co-op. Farms .	6	448	7,521	4,040	71,517	—
W.I. Stalls .	31	7,259	566	3,474	—	—
GRAND TOTAL (B)	89	46,617	—	—	—	—
C. SERVICE SOCIETIES:						
Cattle and Poultry Breeders	8	3,413	27,762	5,492	9,715	—
Seed Growers .	4	337	11,149	996	3,494	17,404
Servicing and Miscellaneous	29	9,879	59,373	71,386	69,891	26
GRAND TOTAL (C)	41	13,629				
„ „ (B)	89	46,617				
„ „ (A)	87	76,618				
	217	136,864				

* As shown by Societies' returns to the Registrar of Friendly Societies in Marcl

XVIII

ENGLAND ONLY, 1948 : TABLE OF RETURNS *

Dairy	*Eggs and Poultry*	*Meat, Bacon, Livestock*	*Wool*	*Fruit and Vegetables*	*Seeds*	*Unclassified*	*Total Turnover in £s*
—	—	—	—	—	—	—	119,894
—	—	—	—	—	—	5,510	290,753
—	4,970	—	—	—	—	68,934	1,038,638
—	—	—	20,554	4,101	—	267,929	2,934,025
—	—	1,505	—	—	—	420,720	3,757,761
—	21,270	—	—	—	—	1,367,115	6,670,423
284,352	1,882,616	—	7,140	422,863	—	1,501,296	8,919,038
—	—	—	—	—	—	—	23,730,532
615,302	—	—	—	—	—	3,483	618,786
—	6,291,414	—	—	791	—	580,565	6,887,742
2,361	27,197	42,207	—	776	380	20,651	93,672
—	—	1,313,769	—	—	—	39,140	1,352,909
—	—	—	161,344	—	—	618	162,024
—	30,703	—	—	1,308,107	—	1,173,978	2,693,315
12,156	4,618	5,952	—	47,138	4,181	5,939	79,978
287	1,028	—		25,576	—	43,799	70,690
—	—	—	—	—	—	—	11,959,116
—	588	—	—	—	—	47,592	48,180
—	—	—	—	—	—	34,789	52,193
—	—	—	—	—	—	154,432	154,458
							254,831 11,959,116 23,730,532
							£35,944,479

1949 (excludes Welsh and Scottish Societies).

the C.W.S. belongs. In Ireland, the farmers' Co-operatives won the battle for control of the creameries and of their own marketing only in the face of persistent opposition from the C.W.S., with its deeply rooted 'consumer' outlook. In England, the attempt to transplant Irish methods, under the auspices of the English Agricultural Organisation Society, ended in failure and collapse; and the English farmers' movement has never fully recovered from the blow. For many years the task of federating and representing the English Agricultural Co-operative Societies was left to the National Farmers' Union, through a special Co-operative section. But the N.F.U., dominated by the larger farmers, never showed any enthusiasm for the task.

English Agricultural Co-operation, if it is to make any substantial contribution to the development of the Co-operative movement, will have to fight its own way, without much help from the Co-operative Union or the Consumers' Societies until it has become strong enough to make its own terms. The question is whether it should set out to establish its own agencies for wholesale buying and for direct retail sale to consumers over a much wider field than at present. Should there be a renewed attempt to establish an Agricultural Wholesale Society, on the Irish model, to cover both marketing and collective purchase of farm requirements? Or should the Agricultural Societies make an effort to work in some sort of partnership with the C.W.S. over the whole field? Again, should the Marketing Societies aim at setting up as many as possible of their own retail outlets—shops and market stalls—or should they seek rather to drive bigger and better bargains for the sale of their goods through the local Consumers' Societies? These are questions which I lack the knowledge to answer with any confidence; and accordingly I merely put them forward as problems deserving much more consideration than they commonly get.

CO-OPERATIVE FARMING

Actual Co-operative farming, as distinct from Co-operative marketing, purchase of requirements, and arrangements for the joint use of expensive farming machinery, hardly exists in Great

Britain. There have been quite a number of small experiments, spread over more than a century, but nothing much has come of them. The Agricultural Guild, founded at Welwyn after the First World War, made a promising start, but its experience showed the great difficulties in the way; indeed, it could never have started at all but for the availability of land belonging to the new Garden City, or without the help of the Garden City and of the market provided by its collectively owned distributive store.

Whether there is in this country a future for Co-operative farming by Producers' Societies, as distinct from Societies of Consumers and from Societies for marketing or the purchase of farm requisites, I am very doubtful. If there is, it seems most likely to develop out of State farming rather than directly from the establishment of joint farming enterprises. Should the State institute on any considerable scale experimental State farms of the type repeatedly suggested since the Labour Government of 1929–31 put forward its abortive proposals, such ventures might in the long run be developed into Co-operative concerns. Moreover, if agricultural land were to be made public property and an attempt were to be made under public ownership to re-shape farm holdings, at any rate in certain districts, into better economic units, experiments in Co-operative farming enterprise might well be made in connection with such a development. This entire question is, however, so speculative at present, and discussion of it would lead me so far away from the main theme of this book, that it seems best to leave it alone.

Chapter VIII

WHOLESALING—OTHER TRADES

*

IN 1948 the two Co-operative Wholesale Societies, together with their joint subsidiary which is mainly engaged in the tea trade, had a combined distributive turnover of nearly £308 millions. Their productive departments had manufactured goods to a value of £100 millions. Thus, allowing for the wholesale margin, more than one-third of their total wholesale trade was in goods produced in the factories of the Wholesale Societies. But, of course, the extent of the processing which took place under Co-operative control differed widely from product to product, and, on the average, for each £1 of output the wages paid for productive labour were only about *2s. 6d.* Even goods produced in the Co-operative factories included varying proportions of non-Co-operative production at the earlier stages of manufacture. Thus, well over half the goods sold by the Wholesale Societies were not of their own manufacture, even in part; whereas the major part of the £502 millions of retail trade done by the local Societies was in goods bought from the Wholesales, and a good deal of the rest was either of their own production (£57 millions) or was produced by Federal Societies, such as Dairies and Bakeries, or by the Producers' Societies which sold either through the Wholesales or direct to the local Societies.

CO-OPERATIVE WHOLESALING OUTSIDE THE FOOD TRADES

The trade of the Wholesale Societies is spread over a very wide range of goods. Outside the food trades, the retail Societies sold in 1948 over £43 millions of drapery goods, £25 millions of furniture and hardware, £15 millions of boots and shoes, and nearly £13 millions of tailoring and outfitting goods. Most of these were bought from the Wholesales, or, on a smaller scale, from the Producers' Co-operatives. They also sold £21 millions of coal, £9 millions of chemists' goods, and £13 millions of other goods, excluding tobacco, for which the detailed figures are not available. The Wholesale Societies, then, hold an important place in many branches of wholesale trade outside the food trades, though in most sections their percentage of the total trade done in the country is fairly small.

This means that almost any attempt to reorganise any branch of wholesale distribution, by placing it under unified management responsible to the State, would run up against the strong opposition of the Co-operative movement, if such a proposal meant taking any part of the existing trade of the Wholesale Societies out of their hands. This opposition would extend to the retail Societies, which would be threatened with the loss of the dividends they at present receive on their purchases from the Wholesale Societies. The reorganisation of wholesale distribution under public auspices would not, however, necessarily eliminate Co-operative wholesaling from any branch of trade to which it might be applied. The Wholesales could buy in bulk from the new public marketing agencies and could re-sell to the local Societies, as they do at present where they purchase from private wholesalers and not direct from the manufacturers. They would, however, stand to lose if the new marketing agencies set out to deal directly with the retail outlets, for if such dealings extended to the local Co-operative Societies, these latter would not be in a position to continue to buy from the Wholesale Societies unless these got their supplies from the new agencies at a special rate; whereas, if the new agencies dealt only with the Co-operative Wholesales and not with the local Societies, the Wholesales would have to demand special terms in order to put the local Consumers' Societies in as good a position as their trading rivals which the new agencies were supplying direct. No doubt, these difficulties could be met if the Co-operative Wholesale Societies were given sufficient price discounts on bulk purchases to enable them to meet costs and pay dividends for their member Societies while charging no higher prices than those at which the new agencies supplied their rivals. But for the present, at any rate, any attempt to give the Wholesale Societies a preferred position as buyers would raise intense political controversy. This might not be the case—or might not matter—at a later stage in the development of a system of public enterprise in which the Co-operative movement had acquired a generally recognised place. But Co-operators naturally think more at present about what is likely to happen to their trading ventures in the near future than about what might happen to them in a greatly changed climate of opinion and social structure.

WHOLESALING AND THE 'MUTUALS'

The position would be radically altered if the suggestions made in an earlier chapter for the 'mutualisation' of retail trade had come largely into effect. For in that event the State, instead of setting up its own agencies for the conduct of wholesale trade with the retailers, would have taken over the wholesale buying departments of the big chain and multiple concerns, and would have re-grouped them as central buying agencies for the local 'Mutuals' in the various branches of retail trade. These agencies, operating under State control pending their gradual conversion into quasi-Co-operatives owned by the local 'Mutuals', would act as the principal suppliers of the 'Mutuals', would be in a position to place bulk orders with manufacturers and to encourage the production of standard 'utility lines', and would compete on equal terms with the existing Co-operative Wholesale Societies. They might even establish their own factories, like those of the C.W.S. and S.C.W.S., or might acquire a controlling interest in factories producing exclusively for their requirements. But, even without setting up their own factories or taking over the ownership of existing factories, they would be in a position by virtue of their connections with the local 'Mutuals' to achieve significant reductions in costs.

Indeed, this form of wholesaling would largely dispense with the need for direct State wholesaling of most kinds of consumers' goods outside the trade in food. The need for direct State action arises mainly where special measures are called for to plan home production in relation to imported supplies, and, outside the food trades, this necessity arises mainly in connection with raw or semi-finished materials rather than finished consumers' goods. The State would, no doubt, need to exercise some degree of final control over the wholesale trading operations of the Co-operative Wholesale Societies as well as of the new agencies set up in connection with the 'mutualisation' of retail trade; but the actual trading operations could be left in the hands of these agencies, which could supply the small-scale private traders as well as the Co-operative and 'Mutual' retail outlets.

The problem of the relation of 'State trading' to Co-operative Wholesale trade has not arisen in a serious form hitherto, because where the State has entered the field of wholesale trading it has in most cases been keeping the private wholesalers in existence either by using them as its agents or by treating them as its pensioners where it has actually taken away their functions. This method, however, is exceedingly wasteful, and must be eliminated if the Labour Party is to redeem its promises to cut the margins between the prices paid to producers and those charged to consumers. It is, indeed, one of the main purposes of nationalisation and 'mutualisation' in the field of wholesale trade to get rid of unnecessary payments to middle-men.

Where the State does need, for purposes of co-ordinating home and imported supplies, or in connection with the operation of any sort of subsidy to home producers, to maintain its own primary wholesaling agencies apart from the purchasing bodies connected with the Co-operative movement and with the proposed 'Mutuals', it will be reasonable for it either to deal with the retail trade exclusively through these *media* or, if it sells direct to retailers, to supply the Co-operative and 'Mutual' Wholesale agencies at a lower price in consideration of their bulk orders, and thus to enable them to pay dividends on purchases to the associated retail outlets.

What this amounts to saying is that, if a State trading corporation were to be set up with a monopoly in the right to deal in any commodity, but with power to accept the Co-operative and 'Mutual' Wholesale Societies as main agents for their part of the trade, the Wholesales, in order to justify their being given this position, would have to relieve the State trading agency of enough of the costs of secondary wholesaling to cover the price advantages allowed them.

Before considering the merits of this solution, let us try to see how it would work in practice. Under the suggested arrangement, if the State should wish to set up a unified marketing agency for any product or group of products, it would arrange with the Co-operative Wholesale Societies to act as its distributing agents to all retail Co-operative Societies, allowing a suitable price discount to cover the Wholesale Societies' reasonable trading margin. The State, or an agency set up under its auspices, would thus become the primary wholesaler, marketing the manufacturers' product; the Co-operative movement would keep its position as secondary wholesaler, acting as distributing agency for all Co-operative retail outlets. The 'Mutual' Wholesales would, of course, receive similar treatment.

COAL DISTRIBUTION

What is here in mind can be illustrated most simply by taking the case of coal, where the production is already unified in the hands of a public body, the National Coal Board. The N.C.B. has statutory powers to act as a distributor, dealing directly with the consumers of coal. Before nationalisation, some colliery concerns sold coal direct to bulk consumers, such as electricity generating concerns and factories which used considerable quantities; whereas other collieries had sales subsidiaries which marketed coal for them, and much coal was sold by the collieries to merchants both for export and for home consumption. It seems sensible for the N.C.B. to take over entirely the sale of coal to bulk consumers, not only where these are also public concerns, as in the cases of the railways and of gas and electricity suppliers, but also wherever the quantities are large and the industrial consumers have special requirements in respect of type, quality, and regular delivery. But in dealing with small consumers, including the entire trade in household coal except to large institutions, the Co-operative movement could well take over the function of retailing from the private suppliers, and could make its own collective trading bargain with the N.C.B. concerning the terms of supply, either nationally or, more probably, on a regional or area basis within general terms agreed upon nationally for the entire trade. The Wholesale Societies, to be sure, would not play a large part in such an arrangement—any more than they do at present in the coal trade done by the retail and federal Societies—unless these Societies chose to give the Wholesales a bigger place by using them as agents in buying supplies from the N.C.B.

TOBACCO

In other trades, however, the Wholesale Societies would necessarily play a much larger part. Suppose, for example, as is already the case in a number of countries, the State were to take over the trade in tobacco and administer it, at the wholesale stage, through some sort of Marketing Commission. The entire Co-operative section of the trade could then be handled through the Wholesale Societies, acting as buyers on behalf of the retail Societies and distributing to them in the same way as now. It would then be open to the Wholesale Societies to increase their share in the trade as fast as the retail Societies could expand their sales—receiving of course a discount for bulk handling to cover their services as secondary wholesalers. We shall have to consider later how such an arrangement would affect the Wholesale Societies as *producers* of their own brands and blends, as well as distributors of the various proprietary brands.

DRAPERY

Or take the case of drapery, over the range of goods dealt in by any of the big private wholesale warehouses in London. This is a much more complicated case, because the drapery trade is one in which there is very great scope for rationalisation of manufacture through the development of standard 'lines' and utility specifications and the elimination of varieties that serve no useful purpose, and because the trade is one in which there is a mixture of direct selling by manufacturers and indirect selling through the wholesale houses to the retail shops. The big department stores and chains buy largely direct from the larger manufacturers, and sometimes from the smaller manufacturers as well, especially in the case of 'speciality' goods; whereas the smaller shops buy mainly through wholesale houses, though they may also deal directly with certain manufacturers—again, especially in 'speciality' lines. I am now supposing a situation in which the State has decided to take over, or re-constitute on a new publicly controlled basis, in close connection with the local 'Mutuals', the private wholesale distributing agencies, without interfering with the rights of private manufacturers to sell their products to the retailer direct. In such a case, again, the Co-operative Wholesale Societies could be left to develop their trade, buying either direct from the manufacturers or through the publicly controlled wholesale agencies, as might suit them best; and it would be possible to channel all supplies from the public wholesale agencies to the retail Co-operative Societies through the Co-operative Wholesale Societies, except where the retail Societies preferred to make their purchases direct from the manufacturers.

It would, no doubt, be equally possible for the State, in taking over the function of primary wholesaling, both to forbid direct selling by private manufacturers and to insist on dealing direct with the local Co-operative Societies as well as with other private traders. But in most cases it would be foolish for it to do either of these things. Direct sales by manufacturers have obvious advantages both in the case of 'speciality' lines and in enabling the large retailer to make his own demands upon the manufacturer to meet his particular needs; and the Co-operative movement by channelling its main purchases through the Wholesale Societies will be able to gain the advantages of bulk-buying and to meet economically the demands of the smaller Societies for varied assortments of goods covering a wide range of products.

WHOLESALING AND THE PRODUCTION OF UTILITY GOODS

What has been said of the drapery trade applies in equal measure to a large number of other trades in which there exist similar opportunities for the cutting of costs by the development of standard products and the elimination of varieties which destroy, by making goods unnecessarily expensive, much more consumers' choice than they actually afford. For example, the trade in women's boots and shoes and that in hosiery offer large opportunities for cost-cutting through the placing of bigger orders with manufacturing firms and the greater specialisation of factories in particular styles and qualities. Furniture and furnishings offer similar opportunities, and the part at present played by Board of Trade control in fostering utility production could be largely taken over by re-constituted wholesale agencies, Co-operative or 'Mutual', which set out deliberately to serve the consumers' interests by influencing the course of manufacturing output.

PRIMARY AND SECONDARY WHOLESALING

The problem discussed in the preceding paragraphs clearly involves the distinction, more than once mentioned already, between primary and secondary wholesaling. This distinction, though difficult to draw at some points, is already well recognised in many trades. The primary wholesaler buys from the main producers, at home or abroad, and sells largely in bulk, either to bulk consumers or to secondary wholesalers who supply the retail trade. The two functions—primary and secondary wholesaling—may be combined, and often are to some extent; and, except in case of monopoly, not all trade need pass through either—for the producer may sell direct to the retailer or control his own retail outlets. Where wholesaling is involved as a distinct stage or stages in the passage of goods from producer to consumer, it is not necessarily an economy to concentrate primary and secondary wholesaling in the same hands, especially when the number of separate retail outlets needing to be supplied is very large. It may, for example, be most economical for the primary wholesaling stage to be organised on a specialised basis, so that the primary wholesaler deals only in a relatively narrow range of goods, but to organise secondary wholesaling on a multiple basis, for the supply of mixed consignments covering a wide range of products. Thus the Co-operative Wholesale Societies could continue to act as multiple secondary sales agencies for the diversified demands of the local Co-operatives, even if for some products primary wholesaling were taken over by specialist agencies appointed by a Minister and owned and controlled by the public, either directly or through some form of 'Mutual' organisation.

THE FORM OF PUBLIC TRADING

The attitude of Co-operators to projects for the public re-organisation of primary wholesaling, even if the position of the existing Co-operative agencies were fully safeguarded, would no doubt be much affected by the form given to the agencies set up by the State for this purpose. In my view, such agencies should be given as far and as soon as possible a 'Mutual' or Co-operative form, wherever they are established to handle goods of which the production is mainly in the hands of private firms, as distinct from Public Boards in charge of nationalised industries, such as coal. Where any part of productive industry has been nationalised, it will be natural for the Board which presides over it to act as its own primary wholesaler, and to delegate secondary wholesaling only to approved bodies of which the Co-operative movement would, of course, be one. Where, on the other hand, production remains largely under private ownership and management, the forms of wholesale trading will obviously be affected by the nature and degree of the public control exercised over such industries within the general system of public economic planning. It is therefore unprofitable to attempt to discuss the future of wholesale trading in these fields until some consideration has been given to the probable forms of control over productive industries which fall outside the socialised sector. I shall accordingly come back to this question when I have discussed the place of the Co-operative movement in the sphere of production.

Chapter IX

A SURVEY OF CO-OPERATIVE PRODUCTION

*

IN 1948 the British Co-operative movement, excluding the Agricultural Co-operative Societies, recorded a productive output valued at £175 millions. This compares with a turnover of £503 millions at retail prices in the local Co-operative stores. The productive output can be divided up as follows, according to the type of body responsible for it:

TABLE XIX

CO-OPERATIVE PRODUCTION, 1948*

(*£ thousands*)

(A) By Wholesale Societies:			
Co-operative Wholesale Society	£78,268		
Scottish C.W.S. . . .	23,267		
Joint English and Scottish C.W.S.	1,887		
		£103,422	
(B) By other Federal Societies . .		13,184	
(C) By local Consumers' Societies .		57,046	
By Consumers' Societies .			£173,652
(D) By Producers' Societies . .			£5,118
By all types . . .			£178,790

* Excluding Agricultural Societies

Thus by far the greater part of the total is produced by the two great Wholesale Societies, and most of the remainder by the productive departments of the local Consumers' Societies. The Federal Societies, mostly local or regional federations of Consumers' Societies, come third; and the Producers' Societies bring up the rear, with only a tiny fraction of the total output.

TABLE XX

Co-operative Production in 1948. Food and Drink

(*£ thousands*)

	*C.W.S.**	*Joint C.W.S.*	*S.C.W.S.*	*Federal*	*Local*	*Productive*	*Total*
Grain Milling .	11,999	—	4,070	—	—	—	16,069
Baking (including Biscuits)	1,107	—	—	4,650	?	71	5,828+?
Sugar Confectionery .	924	—	1,424	—	?	—	2,348+?
Preserved Foods	7,258	—	139	—	—	—	7,397
Dairy and Milk Products .	14,914	—	3,148	3,847	?	—	21,909+?
Margarine .	3,967	—	276	—	—	—	4,243
Meat and Meat Products .	479	—	1,046	—	?	—	1,525+?
Fish-curing .	—	—	543	—	—	—	543
Cattle, etc., Foods .	855	—	—	—	—	—	855
Soft Drinks and Vinegar .	583	—	232	—	—	—	815
Coffee . .	—	383	438	—	—	—	821
Cocoa and Chocolate .	—	543	—	—	—	—	543
Tea (Estate Output) .	—	961	—	—	—	—	961
	42,086	1,887	11,316	8,497	?	71	63,857+?

* Not including farm output of £1,472,000

The crude figures, however, give a misleading impression of the production carried on under the auspices of the local Consumers' Societies; for a considerable part of what is described in their returns as production should more properly be called 'services'. It is unfortunately not possible to break up the totals so as to show the items separately. Agricultural output of Consumers' Societies, as we saw, accounted for about £1 million. The rest, as far as it was production rather than services, was made up mainly of baking and confectionery-making, tailoring, boot and shoe repairing, building and woodworking; on the

TABLE XXI

Co-operative Production in 1948. Textiles, Clothing and Leather

(*£ thousands*)

	C.W.S.	*S.C.W.S.*	*Federal*	*Local*	*Productive*	*Total*
Textiles and Hosiery .	3,489	1,893	—	—	284	5,666
Tailoring, Dressmaking, etc. .	1,427	561	—	?	1,694	3,682+?
Underwear and Overalls .	1,750	248	—	—	141	2,139
Fellmongery .	499	—	—	—	—	499
Leather and Leather Goods	450	22	—	—	—	472
Boots and Shoes	3,209	572	96*	?	2,125	6,002+?
	10,824	3,296	96*	?	4,244	18,460+?

* Repairing

'services' side it included restaurant and hotel services, funeral undertaking, and laundrying, as well as some marginal undertakings in the working up of products for retail distribution. If the 'service' side is left out, the total value of all Co-operative production in 1948 was probably about £150 millions.

We have next to see broadly how this total was made up. Much the biggest items were in the manufacture and preparation of foodstuffs.

Thus, food and drink, exclusive of the output of the local Consumers' Societies, accounted for nearly £64 millions, or roughly half the productive output of all the other types of Co-operative Society. The next largest group consists of textiles and tailoring, with which I have grouped boots and shoes and other leather goods.

The remaining productive output of the Co-operative Societies in 1948 was made up of the following:

TABLE XXII

CO-OPERATIVE PRODUCTION IN 1948. OTHER PRODUCTS
(*£ thousands*)

	C.W.S.	*S.C.W.S.*	*Federal*	*Local*	*Productive*	*Total*
Tobacco	6,648	5,006	—	—	—	11,654
Printing and Bookbinding	1,654	713	560*	—	401	3,328
Furniture and Upholstery	2,949	856	—	—	—	3,805
Other Woodwork	243	—	—	—	—	243
Brushes	267	27	—	—	—	294
China and Earthenware	92	—	—	—	—	92
Glass	665	—	—	—	—	665
Optical Goods	111	—	—	—	—	111
Chemicals and Soap	6,460	1,413	105	—	—	7,978
Metals and Vehicles	2,513	272	—	—	326	3,111
Building and Contracting	2,282	—	—	?	50	2,332+?
Funeral Undertaking	—	?	132	?	—	132+?
Laundrying, Dyeing and Cleaning	—	368	3,022	?	—	3,390+?
Miscellaneous	—	—	772	?	26	798+?
	23,884	8,655	4,591	?	803	37,933+?

* Co-operative Printing Society

In the above Table I have grouped the Co-operative Printing Society with the Federal Societies, as it properly belongs there rather than in the Productive group, being owned mainly by local Consumers' Societies and not controlled by its employees. A number of other Productive Societies are partly owned by Consumers' Societies, but have mostly an element of producers' control. Not quite all of them, however, belong to the Co-operative Productive Federation, which is the national agency of the Producers' Societies. In the following Table, the figures for the Societies belonging to the C.P.F. are set out separately.

TABLE XXIII

PRODUCTION OF CO-OPERATIVE PRODUCTIVE SOCIETIES IN 1948

(*£ thousands*)

	C.P.F.	*Others*	*Total*
Clothing and Allied Trades . .	2,119	—	2,119
Footwear and Allied Trades . .	2,125	—	2,125
Printing and Allied Trades . .	255	707	962
Building and Allied Trades . .	40	—	40
Metal and Vehicle Trades . .	326	—	326
Other Trades	110	10	120
	4,975	717	5,692

Adding the various groups together, we get the totals given in Table XXIV, p. 130.

It will be seen from Tables XIX to XXIV that production by Co-operative Societies is spread over a wide range of industries, but does not in any case account for a large proportion of the total national output. The largest items in the Co-operative total are flour-milling and milk and dairy products; next to these stand preserved foods, tobacco and chemicals (including soap, which is the biggest item). There is very little Co-operative production in the textile industries, except hosiery; but the manufacture of clothing is important and includes a substantial contribution from the Producers' Societies. Baking and laundrying are among the main activities of local Consumers' Societies and local Federations; and tea-blending, which has not been counted as 'production' for the purpose of the Tables, is carried on upon a large scale by the Joint Wholesale Society. Outside these fields the Co-operative contribution to national output is comparatively small.

It is, indeed, non-existent in many branches of industry. Generally speaking, the Co-operative Societies produce only goods for which there is a regular and assured sale in the retail consumers' market, and concentrate largely on the later stages of

TABLE XXIV

CO-OPERATIVE PRODUCTION IN 1948. PRINCIPAL PRODUCTS

(*£ thousands*)

	C.W.S.	*Joint C.W.S.*	*S.C.W.S.*	*Federal*	*Local*	*Productive*	*Total*
Food	41,503	—	10,646	8,497	?	71	60,717+?
Drink	583	1,887	670	—	—	—	3,140
Tobacco	6,648	—	5,006	—	—	—	11,654
Textiles and Clothing	6,666	—	2,702	—	?	2,119	11,487+?
Boots and Leather	4,158	—	594	96*	?	2,125	6,973+?
Printing, etc.	1,654	—	713	560†	—	401	3,328
Furniture and Woodwork	3,192	—	856	—	—	—	4,048
Glass and Pottery	757	—	—	—	—	—	757
Chemicals and Soap	6,460	—	1,413	105	—	—	7,978
Metals and Vehicles	2,513	—	272	—	—	326	3,111
Building and Contracting	2,282	—	—	—	?	50	2,332+?
Laundries, Dyeing and Cleaning	—	—	368	3,022	?	—	3,390+?
Miscellaneous	378	—	27	904	?	26	1,335+?
	76,794	1,887	23,267	13,184	57,046	5,118	177,296

* Not including farm output of £1,472,000
† Including Co-operative Printing Society

manufacture: so that there is in many cases a considerable non-Co-operative element in the value of Co-operative products. In the case of flour-milling, the Wholesale Societies do manufacture on a big scale an intermediate product for further processing by Federal and Local Consumers' Societies; but this is an exceptional case. The only other instances in which production is not mainly for the consumers' market are building and vehicle building, which are both undertaken mainly for the internal purposes of the movement.

Thus, Co-operative production is almost non-existent in the basic industries, such as iron and steel and the various branches of engineering. It does not extend at all to builders' materials: there is no Co-operative manufacture of bricks, or of cement, or of builders' metalwork or woodwork. There are no Co-operatively produced heavy chemicals, as distinct from soap and drugs. The Co-operative share in the cotton and woollen industries is very small and highly specialised; there is no Co-operative production of rayon or of other textile substitutes. In effect, Co-operation, as a productive agency, has no, or almost no, place in any of the productive industries which are, or have been recently, seriously considered as possible candidates for early nationalisation, with the single, but important, exception of flour-milling. Even in the case of milling, the number of Co-operative employees in 1948 was less than 2,500, out of 40,000 employed in the industry. In the clothing trades, which accounted for the largest number of Co-operative employees engaged in production in any group, the total was well under 12,000, out of a labour force of 474,000. In the furniture trades it was about 3,700 out of 118,000; in printing, about 3,600 out of 313,000; in the boot and shoe industry, about 6,200 out of 148,000; in the tobacco trades, under 1,000 out of 49,000. These are all examples of industries in which Co-operative production is substantial; in most others the proportion of Co-operative to total employment is much smaller still.

Measured in terms of the numbers employed, the average Co-operative factory is fairly small, as one would expect from the character of the trades carried on. In the case of the Co-operative Wholesale Society, the average in most trades is from 300 to 400 employees, tailoring factories being the biggest, with an average of 500, and textile and metal-working establishments among the smallest, with about 200 workers. The factories of the Productive Societies tend to be rather smaller. Their average for clothing is about 350, for boots and shoes 120, and for printing only 80. The figures for the Scottish C.W.S. are more difficult to analyse, because the Scottish policy has been to concentrate production largely on the Shieldhall Estate at Glasgow. In the case of textiles and clothing, the Scottish average is as high as 800 employees. There are no really huge Co-operative establishments, employing thousands of workers. There are, however, some very highly mechanised establishments—for example, in flour-milling—in which the number of employees does not furnish a satisfactory measure of scale.

Chapter X

THE FUTURE OF CO-OPERATIVE PRODUCTION

*

It is evident, in the light of the foregoing survey, that the Co-operative movement neither is, nor is likely to be for a long time to come, in a position to take over, or even to assume the predominant place in the conduct of, any manufacturing industry, apart from flour-milling, which we have considered already. Spokesmen of the movement sometimes talk as if a convenient line could be drawn between basic industries and services, which are suitable for nationalisation, and consumers' industries, which should fall within the legitimate sphere of Co-operative enterprise. But this is sheer nonsense, if it is meant to imply that the existing movement of either Consumers' or Producers' Co-operation, or the two together, are nearly in a position to supersede capitalist enterprise in any considerable branch of manufacturing production. The most Co-operators can look for in practice, or are at all inclined to aim at in point of fact, is an increased output of certain kinds of goods for which there is a steady and sufficient market in the local Co-operative Stores, leaving to other agencies the supplying of the greater part of the national demand. This leaves a very considerable field open; but it is entirely unrealistic to look forward, at any future date that is worth thinking about, to a situation in which the existing Co-operative movement will have become, by its own internal expansion, the principal producer in any important branch of consumers' industry.

Discarding such pipe-dreams, let us concentrate our attention on the part the Co-operative movement can reasonably look forward to playing in the productive activity of the 'collectivist economy' on which we are entering. In order to do this, it is necessary to make certain assumptions, or forecasts, concerning the changes in industrial structure that are likely to result from the successive tenure of office of, say, three or four more Labour Governments backed by sufficient parliamentary majorities. How many industries and services are we to expect such Governments to 'nationalise', in the sense of taking them—or the major part of them—out of private ownership and transferring them to some form of State management, either by Public Boards or by some other device for combining managerial autonomy with effective responsibility to the public and sufficient conformity with the requirements of national economic planning? Over how many additional industries will such Governments be likely, without full nationalisation, to set up some form of Development Council or Control Board, exercising considerable powers of regulation in the interests of national planning and amenability to the needs of the public? What form are such controlling agencies likeliest to take, and what will be the position of the individual businesses in the industries concerned in relation to them? Will there be one way of dealing with large businesses or combines, and another of dealing with relatively small concerns? Will the State, where an industry is not nationalised as a whole, take over and run as public enterprises some of the key firms? Will it acquire a share- or debenture-holding interest in yet others, and run them as 'mixed' enterprises, under a system of combined public and private control? What part will it play, as the further diminution of economic inequality reduces the availability of private capital for investment, in directing the flow of capital resources out of public funds; and how far will it use its influence over the supply of capital to encourage one form of business enterprise rather than another?

NATIONALISATION AND THE ALTERNATIVES

To answer these questions at all fully would require an entire book—and one that would be, at this stage, exceedingly difficult to write. For nobody has yet thought out at all clearly the answers to most of them. No doubt, many members of the Labour Party have been accustomed to thinking of 'nationalisation' as a process that would go on and on, beginning with the most obvious cases and then proceeding in an ever-widening circle of which the circumference is left undefined. But I doubt if this is how most of the Labour Party's leaders now envisage the future, or if any realistic economist, no matter how strong his Socialist convictions, takes such a view. The plain fact is that, when iron and steel have joined the existing group of nationalised industries and services, it will not be at all easy to find more than a few others[1] that are at all suitable for being taken over in the same way as was employed by the Labour Government of 1945–50 in carrying through its extensive programme of socialisation.

There are two main reasons why not much further progress can well be made without a change of method. The first is that most of the major industries now left in private hands are much more diversified, and are made up of many more separate firms doing a wide range of different things, than the industries so far transferred to public operation. The engineering and textile industries, for example, are made up of hosts of firms, of all sorts and sizes, producing under widely different conditions and for a great variety of markets. To nationalise the engineering industry would be a colossal task; and a National Board put in charge of running it would be utterly overwhelmed. Even if it were broken up, on the analogy of the transport industry, and put under a number of separate Executives tied together by a co-ordinating Engineering Commission, the difficulties of demarcation between the branches would be immense and in many of them the number of separate units would be quite unmanageably large. Or take the case of textiles. Even if each textile industry—cotton manufacture, woollen and worsted manufacture, silk, rayon, hosiery, bleaching and dyeing, and the rest—were treated as a separate affair, the number and diversity of the units would make the conduct of each as a unified national business very difficult indeed, however much attempt might be made to push decentralisation to the farthest possible point.

Secondly, it would be undesirable, even if it were practicable, to force the wide diversity of businesses of all sorts and sizes which make up the general run of British manufacturing industry

[1] E.g. shipbuilding.

into the strait-jacket of a series of sectional monopolies, even under public ownership. In the interests of technical progress and of finding new ways of catering for consumers' wants, it is expedient to leave room for the starting of new businesses, without making it necessary for them to be set on foot as branches of existing great concerns or subjecting them to the control of those in charge of processes which they may be destined to supersede. It will be a poor world in which a man with an idea cannot get a chance of trying it out without needing the sanction and accepting the discipline of some vast national organisation that may well look on him either as a dangerous competitor or as a crank. We want more and not fewer chances for small-scale enterprise in producing new commodities or adopting new methods; and the pattern of socialisation needs to be elastic enough to make room for the innovator and for the man who cannot be happy under the discipline of a great machine.

Both these issues have already arisen in connection with the nationalisation of iron and steel. The whole industry is not taken over under the Act: public ownership is limited to the basic sections, together with those subsidiary enterprises which cannot economically be divorced from them. Moreover, in the nationalised sections, the separate firms taken over are for the present to keep their identity, and are not to be converted into mere branches of a single gigantic operating concern. In the case of steel, there is a clearly marked nucleus of the whole industry—the crude and semi-finished steel-producing plants—which supplies the essential materials both for the finishing sections and for a number of other industries, and needs to be nationalised because of its key position in the entire national economy. If this nucleus is in public hands, together with a sufficient part of the finishing section to rule out the possibility of dangerous restrictive monopoly practices in the remainder, the essential requirements of national planning and responsible control are satisfied without the need to take over the whole industry.

But in most manufacturing industries there is no similar clearly marked key section that can be taken into public hands. In the cotton industry, no doubt the preparing and spinning of cotton yarn occupy to some extent an analogous position, and could be taken over together with such weaving as is done in combined factories, the rest of the weaving and finishing being left to private firms. But in most of the other textile industries and in most branches of engineering and metal-working there are no corresponding key sections. There are, however, both in these and in many other industries, certain individual key *firms* which by virtue of their control of certain processes or patents exert an influence over a wide field—for example, as suppliers of patent machinery or of some vital material or component. It may be much more to the point to make these particular firms fully amenable to public control than to take over the main part of the industries or groups to which they belong; and the forms of socialisation ought to be varied enough to make this possible wherever the case for it can be fairly made out.

I am not denying that there do still remain a number of industries which it may be desirable for the State to take over entirely, or nearly so; but I believe there are not many of them. In my opinion they include, among major industries, ship-building, shipping, aircraft production, the production of non-ferrous metals, and also the manufacture of some of the key materials used in building. To these I would add cotton spinning, and possibly the production of rayon and staple fibre; and I have already suggested flour-milling and sugar manufacture as industries suitable for complete socialisation under conditions which would allow the Co-operative movement a substantial share in their conduct.

Beyond this I do not find it easy to go in advocating the taking over of entire industries, or even of the major part. But there are a number of other industries in which I should like to see large sections nationalised, while competing businesses were left in private hands. Examples are motor-car manufacture—of standardised, relatively cheap vehicles only; building and civil engineering—the big contracting firms only, in the first instance: certainly not the host of small jobbing builders; heavy chemicals—in effect by the public acquisition of Imperial Chemical Industries as a going concern; oil-refining; rubber; agricultural machinery making—only the big firms. Then there are other cases in which there are strong reasons for taking over particular concerns that are in possession of powerful monopolies—the making of machinery for the boot and shoe industry, for example, and certain branches of electrical engineering. Finally, there is also a case for either taking over a limited number of existing businesses or setting up new ones under public ownership for the purpose of direct competition in branches of production which are to be left mainly in private hands. Such public concerns could be used to prevent monopolistic trade practices, to try out new methods, and to set standards by which to judge the achievements of the private firms.

When all this had been done, the greater part of manufacturing industry would still be left outside the range of national ownership and operation. The vast majority of firms would remain untouched, for most firms are small. In most industries only a small minority of workers would be converted into employees of the public. What, then, would be the position in this large continuing 'private sector'?

STATE CONTROL OF BUSINESS

As I see the outlook, the State would have set up, while these measures of socialisation were being carried through by stages, a system of Development Boards for each of the major industries, with considerable powers and responsibilities. Each Board would consist of an equal number of representatives of the firms and of the Trade Unions in the industry concerned, together with an equal number chosen by the appropriate Minister to represent the public. Over each Board would preside a full-time Chairman, appointed by the Minister after consultation with the rest of the Board. The Minister would be authorised to issue policy directions to the Board, in the same way as in the nationalised industries, except that his powers of direction would need to be more narrowly defined. He would be able to issue binding directions concerning such matters as prices and margins, production of specified utility lines and production for export. His sanction would be needed for all major projects of capital development, including the use of capital reserves. He would be able to veto any restrictive arrangements for price maintenance or allocation of markets; to prescribe, in default of satisfactory action by the Board, standard forms of accounting and costing; to order a special investigation into the affairs of any firm or any branch of the industry. The Development Board would present him with an annual report of its proceedings; and he would present this report to Parliament with his own comments and proposals for action attached.

Such Boards, I suggest, would be set up for each important, clearly definable, industrial group; and any firms within the group that had passed under public ownership would be represented on the Boards in the same way as private firms. Thus, the public representation would increase if and when sections of the industry were taken under public operation. The Minister's representatives on the Boards would include a proportion of full-time experts, some of whom might serve on more than one Board and also as directors of publicly owned firms in the fields of their special knowledge. The full-time Chairmen of related Boards would be able to serve as advisers to the Minister on the issues affecting their mutual relations.

It would not be necessary for all firms in an industry to belong to its Development Board. In many cases the small firms, if they preferred, could be left outside, subject to less onerous obligations than the member firms, and with power to appeal to the Minister against the Board if they considered it to be acting unreasonably. Nor would it be necessary that there should be a Board for every industry, or that every firm should be squeezed into the framework of a particular industry. The object of setting up the Development Boards should be, not to create uniformity or centralise control, but to promote efficiency and co-ordinated effort to meet the consumers' demands with the minimum of control required to achieve such standardisation and specialisation as are really desirable in the interests of low-cost production and economy of man-power, without interfering with either the innovator or the provider for special, diversified wants.

THE SUPPLY OF CAPITAL

The Development Board would be one agency for ensuring the conformity of non-nationalised industries with the requirements of the general economic plan. But there would, I think, be another that is highly relevant to the theme of this discussion. If, under the conditions of the future, room is to be left effectively open for the starting of new businesses of a pioneering sort, or indeed to meet the wishes of those who can do better and happier work in small than in large organisations, much more provision than at present will have to be made both for advances of capital to such businesses and for reducing their capital requirements by enabling them to rent premises and power under the easiest possible conditions. What is now done in these ways to help firms to settle on the few Industrial Trading Estates will have to be done much more generally in all types of area. It will have to be made easy to start a small factory *anywhere*, except where considerations of town and country planning or unavailability of man-power make such developments socially undesirable. The State will have to stand ready both to advance money and to provide buildings for suitable applicants, and it is highly undesirable that the power to give or to refuse help should rest with the firms already in the industry in question, or with the Development Board responsible for that industry. Separate agencies, mainly on a regional or local basis, will be needed to provide the requisite facilities, either on Industrial Trading Estates or elsewhere, and there will need to be a simple, not exacting code of practice to which new firms starting with this sort of assistance will be called upon to conform.

THE PLACE OF CO-OPERATIVE PRODUCTION

How could the Co-operative movement fit, with adequate opportunities for development, into such a structure as I have here outlined? In no case, except flour-milling, would any important existing Co-operative enterprise be affected by any scheme of nationalisation; and in this industry I have suggested that either the entire business should be reorganised as a 'Mutual' enterprise, with strong Co-operative representation, or the Co-operative flour-mills should be left to operate under licence from the Public Board that would be put in charge of the mills transferred from private to public ownership and operation. The nationalisation of the big building and civil engineering firms would not affect the Building Departments of the Co-operative Wholesale Societies or of the local Consumers' Societies; nor would it prevent the establishment of Producers' Co-operatives in this field. For the rest, Co-operative enterprises simply do not exist in the industries which I have designated as likely candidates for nationalisation, either of whole industries or of key sections.

There are, however, a number of Co-operative factories, both under the auspices of the Wholesale Societies and conducted by Producers' Co-operatives, in industries which are likely to be placed under the co-ordinating jurisdiction of Development Boards. In no instance would these factories constitute a large fraction of the industries in question, and their voice in the affairs of the Development Boards would consequently be small. It would be for the Co-operative movement to choose, in each case, whether to bring its establishments within the scope of the Development Boards, or to remain aloof while accepting the general directives issued by the Boards with the sanction of the appropriate Minister. I think that, in most cases, it would be in the movement's best interests to associate itself with the Boards, while reserving its right to appeal to the Minister if it considered that any action was being taken against its interests. Such association would enable the Co-operative movement to stake out its claim for a fair share in projects of capital development, including State aid in financing such projects when the movement could not finance them out of its own resources.

Indeed, I think the Co-operative movement should use its position on the Development Boards, and its national influence, to ensure that as many as possible of the projects involving the establishment of new factories should be given a Co-operative form, either as new ventures of the Wholesale Societies or as Producers' Co-operatives. I can see wide scope for the setting up of new Co-operative factories under development schemes both for the mass-production of standard consumers' goods and for the relatively small-scale production of specialist consumers' products, such as furniture, pianos, various kinds of clothing and household requisites. I can see in addition great opportunities for starting Co-operative factories—especially Producers' Societies—on Industrial Trading Estates or elsewhere, in premises provided by and rented from the public authorities, including New Towns and areas in old industrial districts scheduled for re-development. In these ways there could be set on foot a marriage between publicly provided capital and Co-operative enterprise that could immensely widen the scope for the expansion of Co-operative production on terms that would leave full freedom for Co-operative ventures to develop untrammelled by centralised bureaucratic control.

THE PRODUCERS' SOCIETIES

In these developments, Consumers' and Producers' Co-operation could advance side by side, and with room to expand without jostling. I should like to see many productive ventures set on foot in free partnership between the Trade Unions and the Consumers' Societies, and under the joint control of producers' and consumers' nominees. The Co-operative Wholesale Societies, instead of looking with jealous eyes on the Producers' Co-operatives, ought to be prepared to collaborate with the Trade Unions in fostering such ventures, especially in branches of manufacture in which production can be efficiently carried on in small or medium-sized factories—as in boot-making, in many branches of the clothing industry and in a wide range of other consumers' trades. The State and the local authorities ought to be prepared, as they are in France and Italy, to give contracts to such Producers' Societies—e.g. for the supply of uniform clothing, furniture, kitchen and canteen installations, educational apparatus, printing and office equipment. Another large sphere for the operation of Producers' Co-operatives under joint producer-consumer control would be in popular entertainment and in catering; and there is the largest scope of all in building and civil engineering, which have yielded some of the most notable examples of successful execution of public works by Producers' Co-operatives in many continental countries.

In all these fields the Co-operative movement—Wholesale and Producers' Societies alike—could find wide scope for expansion in a form of partnership with the State that would leave the essential features of Co-operative enterprise intact within the structure of a broadly collectivised economy. Co-operation could expand much faster in these ways, and with much better assurance of consolidating its position in the society of the future, than it can hope to do as long as it clings to its traditional methods and refuses to face the problems that it will have to face as soon as the Labour Party is in a position to make its next considerable step forward. The Co-operative movement was entirely correct in insisting on maintaining its separateness, as a 'State within the the State', as long as the only real alternative open to it was a subordinate partnership with uncontrolled capitalist enterprise. It is under the necessity of revising its attitude now that there exists the alternative of a constructive partnership with the Welfare State.

Chapter XI

CO-OPERATIVE EMPLOYMENT

*

IN the industries which have been nationalised since 1945, joint consultation has been made a statutory obligation. Each National Board is required by law to set up joint consultative machinery at each level, from the individual establishment up to the national administration itself. A similar system of joint consultation exists under the Whitley Scheme in the Post Office and to a less extent in other branches of the Civil Service. There have also been many developments of joint consultative machinery in private industries, from Joint Works and Workshop Committees up to regular arrangements for national consultation between Trade Unions and employers' representatives. In most of these instances joint consultation is still at an inchoate stage; but there is not much doubt that they have come to stay and to develop, and none that consultation will be an important feature of the organisation of every nationalised industry or service.

EMPLOYEE REPRESENTATION

The idea of joint consultation is by no means new to the Co-operative movement. It was discussed at length by the Co-operative Survey Committee which reported during the First World War, and it has been under intermittent discussion ever since. A number of experiments were made locally after the Survey Committee's report, and some others have been made since; but very little has come of them. Consideration of their merits has often got tangled up with the quite different question whether Co-operative employees ought to be represented on Management Committees, or ought without special representation to be allowed to stand as ordinary candidates for election by the general body of members. A few local Co-operative Societies do provide reserved seats for employees, and some others allow employees to stand; but most do neither, and the Co-operative Union's most recent pronouncements on the matter have been hostile to both. It appears to have been the predominant view in the Consumers' Societies that control ought to rest with the consumer-members, and that the employees should have no share in it, their claims being fully met by the recognition of their Trade Unions and by the negotiation with these bodies of agreed wage-rates and conditions of employment.

THE POSITION OF THE SALARIED OFFICERS

Opinion in the Consumers' Societies has been predominantly hostile, not only to employee representation on Management Committees, but also to the choice of salaried officers to serve as representatives of their Societies on federal or national bodies. Representatives of the 'lay' Committees of Management make up the higher committees of the Co-operative Union, right up to the national level: the full-time officers of the Societies are practically excluded from any part in its higher government. Even the full-time directors of the Wholesale Societies are recruited from the 'lay' members, and not from the lesser officials. In these respects the Co-operative and Trade Union movements present a sharp contrast; for the Trades Union Congress General Council consists entirely of full-time Trade Union officials, and most federal Trade Union bodies are also dominated by the full-time leaders of the constituent Unions.

The effect of the Co-operative practice is, as we have seen, to establish a sharp division between the 'lay' and the salaried leadership, and to exclude the latter from any formal share in the making of policy—though of course many salaried managers have in practice great influence in their own Societies. From the standpoint of the 'consumer philosophy' which has held sway since the days of John Mitchell, managers equally with shop assistants, warehousemen and factory employees are hired workers, with no claim to share in the making of Co-operative policy or in the control of the movement.

JOINT CONSULTATION IN THE CO-OPERATIVE MOVEMENT

Of course, this rejection of the right to a share in control, which was claimed for the employees of the movement by many of the early Co-operative idealists, does not involve rejection of the claim to 'consultation'; for consultation and control are not the same thing. The National Coal Board and the other Boards in charge of the nationalised industries accept the right of the workers to 'joint consultation', but keep decisions in their own hands—and so do private employers who have set up systems of joint consultation. On the workers' side, however, there is some disposition to look on joint consultation, not as giving joint control, but as leading towards it, and to look forward to a time when there will develop out of it, by gradual stages, an increasing participation in actual control. Trade Unionists are not agreed in this matter: indeed, only a small minority is much interested; but that minority includes a high proportion of the best and most intelligent workers.

In Co-operative employment there has been hitherto very little pressure from the workers' side for the establishment of joint consultative machinery. Most Co-operative factories employ a high proportion of unskilled and female labour; and the demand for consultation has come chiefly from the skilled workers. Distributive operations do not lend themselves very easily to workshop forms of organisation; nor are shop workers among the types of Trade Unionists who have been most active in pressing such claims. There is, however, perhaps an additional reason why joint consultation has made so little progress in Co-operative employment. In other occupations, the basis of joint consultation is discussion between representatives of the wage-workers and of the salaried managers—or sometimes of a working board of directors who are managers as well. But in the Co-operative Societies with whom are the workers' representatives to consult? If they consult with the salaried management, the decisions will still have to be taken by the 'lay' Management Committee, on which neither group is represented. If they consult with the Management Committee, this will not bring them face to face with the actual managers, who are the persons with whom they need to establish good human relations. In effect, the peculiar structure of consumers' control puts special obstacles in the way of the establishment of effective joint consultation; and it is not surprising that, where it has been tried, often half-heartedly, it has usually failed to work.

It is, indeed, clear that in the local Consumers' Societies joint consultation can be expected to work only if all these elements are brought in. For example, there could be at the departmental level a rather informal committee of departmental managers and workers' representatives, reporting at the higher level of the whole Society to a tripartite committee or council representing the 'lay' Management Committee, the salaried officers and the rest of the employees. District, Sectional and National Consultation could be built up on this tripartite basis at every level, with the Trade Unions responsible for the workers' representation, the societies of Co-operative Officials for the managerial members, and the appropriate groupings of the Co-operative Union for the representation of the 'consumers'. On such a basis, joint consultation might work on the distributive side of the movement.

On the factory side, as far as the productive establishments of the Wholesale Societies are concerned, there is no reason why the ordinary bipartite structure should not serve; for in this field there is no such sharp divorce between 'lay' committee-men and salaried managers as exists in the local Societies. But consultation will not work unless the directors of the Wholesales bring in the departmental managers and give them the main job of running their own consultative machinery in the various factories and departments. In Federal Societies, such as the Co-operative Printing Society and the United Co-operative Baking Society in Scotland, the complication of the 'lay' committee reappears, and a tripartite structure seems again to be needed.

THE PRODUCERS' SOCIETIES

The Producers' Societies stand, of course, on an entirely different footing, since they do not rest on the theoretical foundation of 'consumers' control'. In their case, a form not merely of joint consultation but of actual joint control exists, through the presence of employee-directors side by side with others appointed to represent the shareholders—including the shareholding Consumers' Societies. The change most needed here seems to be the inclusion of at any rate one or two directors appointed locally or nationally by the Trade Unions in which the workers are enrolled—and, of course, the establishment of effective joint consultation in the actual *workshops*, where it does not already exist. The lack of any organic connection with the Trade Unions has been, ever since the 1870s, a great weakness of the Producers' Societies, which could have provided a laboratory for working out in advance many of the problems of industrial democracy the Trade Unions are now having to face in industry generally and particularly in the nationalised industries.

A CHALLENGE TO THE CO-OPERATIVE MOVEMENT

At some stage the Co-operative movement will have to face the implications of the demand for democracy in industry as it affects their own movement. If they are to claim successfully that Co-operative enterprise satisfactorily meets the requirements of socialisation and is to be ranked with State and municipal enterprise as a form of 'public ownership', they will have to accord to the movement's employees a status in no wise inferior to that which is, or may be in future, accorded to the employees of nationalised concerns. This involves at the very least the establishment, side by side with the existing procedures for collective bargaining, of a system of joint consultation not less favourable or wide in scope than has been set up in, say, the mining industry or the Post Office. It involves working out such a system in close collaboration with U.S.D.A.W.* and the other Trade Unions concerned, and applying it to the warehouses and factories of the Wholesale Societies as well as to the local distributive Societies.

* The Union of Shop Distributors and Allied Workers, which organises the main body of Co-operative employees.

This is an essential first step, without which the Trade Unions and the Labour Party cannot be expected to accept the Co-operative claim that the movement meets the immediate requirements of industrial democracy.

It is, however, only a first step; for it is not to be expected that the methods of joint consultation that have been introduced in the nationalised industries will stand still. On the assumption that full employment is to remain the basis of public economic policy, and that it will never again be possible to enforce steady hard work by the fear of dismissal, or to rely on the incentives characteristic of capitalism for getting an efficient response from the main body of the workers, joint consultation will be bound, as the workers gain experience in it, to develop into something more—into something that will involve a real participation in the taking of decisions affecting the workers' lives and conditions of work. Exactly how this change will come about nobody yet knows. The Trade Unions themselves are uncertain about it, and fearful that, if they involve themselves in responsibility for the efficient conduct of industry, they may forfeit some part of their power to protect their members' interests. But at the same time there exist both a widespread feeling among the keener and more intelligent Trade Unionists that industrial democracy must involve the winning of a higher status in industry and of a growing measure of self-government in the hands of the actual working groups in factories and other places of employment, and also a growing sense among industrial psychologists and students of industrial relations that there is danger of the entire momentum of production slowing down disastrously unless the motive of free and responsible service can be successfully invoked to replace the obsolescent drives of capitalist exploitation.

The Co-operative movement ought to be, not among the hindmost, but in the vanguard of experimentation in the new phase of industrial relations. It ought not to be waiting for the Trade Unions to press it to adopt a new attitude to its employees: it ought to be eager to show that it stands for the most progressive and democratic managerial techniques. But of such an attitude it has so far shown no sign.

CO-OPERATIVE MANAGEMENT

Why Co-operation is thus backward in a matter vital to its future and to the future of British industry as a whole I have already made some attempt to explain. In face of the division that exists between 'lay' Management Committees and salaried managers and officials the responsibility for good and progressive industrial relations is not placed squarely anywhere, and the entire matter is apt to fall between two stools. The 'lay' Committees are dominated by the notion of exclusive consumers' control; and the managers, already subject to this 'lay' control, do not want to encourage workers' participation at the risk of being caught with insufficient authority between two sets of masters. Trade Union pressure is not strong, except on wage issues, largely because of the high proportion of less skilled workers employed in the majority of Co-operative factories—except in the Producers' Societies. Finally, the Wholesale directors, though they become full-time managerial employees, carry with them into their work the exclusive 'consumers' control' attitude which they have learnt during their previous experience as active laymen on Management Committees and on the various committees of the Co-operative Union.

Even apart from the reluctance to adopt progressive techniques in labour relations, there is, I feel sure, something rather badly wrong with Co-operative management. There are, of course, good men in the service of the Co-operative Societies, both wholesale and retail; but is the average level even as good as that of the more progressive capitalist industries—for example, engineering? Frankly, I doubt it; and it would be surprising, in view of all the conditions, if it were as good. There are quite a number of reasons why it should not be. First and most obviously, Co-operative bodies pay low salaries in comparison with capitalist enterprises of comparable scale. Secondly, they recruit their higher officials largely from the ranks of their own employees, and recruit these employees in the first instance, usually at an early age, from those who leave school without a higher education. Thirdly, they give their managers less authority than private capitalist concerns, and subject them to much more detailed lay control. Fourthly, most branches of Co-operative production and also much Co-operative retailing is done under conditions which do not give as easy scope for initiative and the adoption of new techniques as can be found in the more scientifically based industries or in forms of shopkeeping that are concerned with less standardised and less regularly purchased kinds of goods.

It may be answered that the Co-operative movement does not want to imitate the methods of capitalism more than it sheerly must, and that it prides itself on drawing its higher officials from the rank and file of its employees and on *not* paying them salaries far in excess of the earnings of most of the members. I agree that there is much to be said for this point of view, if it can be reconciled with efficiency and progress. But, if the Co-operative movement thinks it can do without more than a very few men who have received a higher education, why do Co-operators show quite as much zeal as other people to procure a higher education for their own children and to promote more democratic access to the higher schools and Universities? Surely, just as in the nationalised industries the need is recognised for a right balance of entrants at different ages and for the recruitment of higher technical and administrative staffs largely from those who have received the appropriate kinds of higher education, so equally the Co-operative movement ought to accept the necessity of a balanced recruitment.

TRAINING FOR CO-OPERATIVE LEADERSHIP

This does not mean that the opportunity of promotion to the highest offices should be denied to those who have left school early and entered into Co-operative employment. But it does mean that, if such promotion is to achieve the right results, the promising young Co-operative employee must be given the fullest opportunities for pursuing his higher education, not merely in his spare time, but with ample release, including where desirable long periods of release with maintenance scholarships that will make it possible to take full-time courses at Technical

Colleges or Universities or other institutions of higher education. No doubt, something is being done to provide opportunities at the Co-operative College; but for how many, and for how long? Moreover, a single College cannot—and could not if it were many times as big as the Co-operative College—provide more than a fraction of the types of courses that are needed to give the many and diverse forms of higher training required in the Co-operative movement. Nor would it be good, even if it were possible, to isolate all the men who were to take higher courses in order to fit them for key positions in Co-operative management in a single institution away from other students, and also, necessarily, away from most of the best teachers in their particular fields of study.

The Co-operative movement has never taken seriously the training of its own men for technical and administrative positions of the kinds needed for a great democratic structure that ought to aim at least as high as the best of capitalist industry. Nor can it put this defect right, save in an isolated instance here and there, by attracting into its service men who have already made their mark in capitalist employment; for it is seldom prepared to pay salaries large enough to draw the best of such 'outsiders'; nor do they always settle down happily in the very different environment of 'lay' consumers' control.

It is, of course, much easier to point out these shortcomings than to propound remedies. One partial remedy is, however, so obvious as to stare one in the face. The Co-operative movement needs to reconsider its entire attitude to the *higher* education and training of its employees, and to be prepared to spend on it at least ten times what it is spending to-day—quite apart from what it needs to spend on better educational opportunities for its members generally.

CO-OPERATIVE SALARIES

A second remedy is to pay higher salaries—not the extravagant salaries paid to a limited group of big capitalist managers, but salaries corresponding to those paid in, say, the Civil Service, as distinct from the recently nationalised industries which have taken over capitalist standards. I do not hesitate to accuse Co-operative Societies of positive meanness in dealing with salary questions; that is indeed one of the sharpest marks of the persistence of the parochial outlook. It is easy to understand in view of the movement's history, but it is not consistent either with its present needs, or with its claim to rank as a proper democratic alternative to nationalisation.

MANAGERS AND COMMITTEES

Thirdly, I feel sure that Co-operative Management Committees in most cases interfere unduly with matters of day-to-day management and administration. It is recognised nowadays that management is a technical job, and that managers cannot be expected to give of their best if someone is continually looking over their shoulders. When Co-operative Societies were small and had few employees, it was natural for the 'lay' Committee to manage the store; indeed, its members often took their turn to serve in it behind the counter and to do the buying. But to-day it is entirely inappropriate for a Committee of spare-time laymen to attempt to *manage* a great business with numerous branches and departments. The proper function of the 'lay' Committee is to appoint the chief managers and to issue general directions about important matters of policy—and, having done that, to give the professional management its head. The Committee should not concern itself with minor appointments, or with the day-to-day running of its stores and departments; having appointed the managers and given them their broad directions, it should come in further, in respect of management, only as a court of appeal when something has gone wrong. If it attempts more than this, it does not give its salaried officers a fair chance.

Moreover, if the Committee insists on trying to manage the stores and departments, it prevents the managers from building up among themselves and with the rest of the employees that team spirit on which, under the conditions of to-day and to-morrow, efficiency is bound to depend. Given a freer hand, the managers could much more easily establish effective systems of joint consultation and group working; and the employees, instead of trying to capture the Committees at elections, would be much more likely to devote their attention to building up satisfactory working relations with the managerial staffs—which is the way to get a happy, effective team. Of course, Management Committees should instruct their managers to make the fullest use of joint consultative techniques. That is part of their business. And, as I have suggested earlier, they should be represented on the central Joint Consultative Committees of their Societies. But, at shop and departmental levels, they should leave the managers and the workers to run joint consultation without them.

ARE CO-OPERATIVE METHODS UP TO DATE?

I am well aware that what I have written in this chapter will annoy many active Co-operators—especially many members of Management Committees. But I hope they will sufficiently overcome their annoyance to ask themselves fairly and squarely the question whether they really believe that the methods they have inherited from a Co-operative movement that was on an altogether smaller scale and was working under much less exacting conditions of scientific and technical knowledge are fully appropriate to the circumstances of the present day, or to the claims which they are advancing that Co-operation must be ranked as the partner of nationalisation, or even as its superior, in the structure of the new 'collectivist economy'. If they answer this question in the affirmative, I must put them another. By what miracle do they suppose that Co-operation alone can stand still in a changing world, resting content for its ten million members and with its assured £500,000,000 of turnover with much the same methods of organisation as it used for running a few grocery shops with a turnover of a few hundred pounds a year?

Chapter XII

CONCLUSION

*

THE British Co-operative movement grew up and assumed its present form in hard times. Its formative years after 1844 fell in a period dominated by the philosophy of 'self-help' and *laissez-faire*. Apart from the Poor Law, there were no public social services at all in the modern sense; and the recently 'reformed' Poor Law was administered with a harshness that was all the more extreme because it was upheld on severe grounds of economic principle. It was held, by the vast majority of those who possessed the vote, that it was a man's duty to support himself and his dependants without help from the State, and that thrift and industry would be fatally undermined if benevolent persons were allowed 'to let hard cases make bad law'. Instances of unmerited misfortune were admitted to exist, but they were regarded as exceptional and as calling for relief by private charity, with only the deterrent hardships of the Poor Law in reserve. It was a man's duty to earn his keep and to put aside out of his earnings, however low, something to support him in illness, unemployment and old age. Mutual thrift agencies among the poor were encouraged with this purpose; laws were passed to stimulate the growth of Friendly Societies and to protect their funds. Co-operative Societies got their first legal recognition as thrift agencies, and were well received by Parliamentarians because they were looked on in this light.

In the prevailing atmosphere of 'economic liberalism', the Co-operative movement was bound to develop entirely apart from the State, to which it looked only for freedom to go its own way with adequate legal protection for its funds. It grew up, side by side with the Friendly Societies, the popular Savings Banks and the Building Societies, as an agency for the 'frugal investment' of working-class savings; and it attracted mainly the thriftier among the workers, belonging for the most part to the more skilled and regularly employed strata of the working class. As it developed, it grew a philosophy to suit its circumstances—a philosophy widely different from that of its first great leader, Robert Owen. For whereas Owen had looked forward to a revolutionary change in the very structure of society, involving the entire supersession of capitalist individualism and competition by a new order based on common ownership and community living, the Co-operators of the period after Rochdale came to accept the existence of capitalist society and to limit their practical ambition to making their movement, as they said, 'a State within the State'. Co-operation, re-founded on the Rochdale principles of dividends on purchases and individual ownership of fixed-interest-bearing share capital, set out to establish its position within the capitalist environment rather than as its antagonist, and, stressing the 'voluntary principle' on which it rested, resigned all claim to make an end of capitalism except by a very gradual process of beating it at its own game.

This insistence on 'voluntarism' as the very basis of the movement was wholly in accord with the spirit of the time. It fitted in with the contemporary idea of the State as existing for a narrowly limited range of purposes, not the least of which was to keep its hands off economic affairs. Given a State which repudiated all responsibility for the economic welfare of the people and referred them to their own personal efforts for meeting every contingency of life, the poorer classes could respond only by building up their own institutions for these purposes—Trade Unions to improve wages and conditions, Friendly Societies to provide benefits in ill-health and old age, Co-operative Societies to guard them against adulteration, to cheapen the costs of living, and to act as investment agencies for their small savings. In fulfilling these purposes, the Co-operative movement rendered magnificent service to a growing fraction of the working class—service which could not, in the circumstances, have been rendered in any other way. But it is none the less true that the foundation of voluntary membership and strict apartness from the State on which the modern Co-operative movement has been built was not so much chosen by Co-operators in preference to any open alternative as forced upon them by the contemporary climate of opinion and by the absence of any State with which they could possibly have established collaborative relations.

The basis of Co-operation had to be voluntary membership: there was nothing else it could be. Co-operators had to manage their affairs apart from the State: there was no point of contact between their affairs and the State's. Except for a few Factory Acts limited to women and children, the State did nothing to regulate industry; it did nothing at all to regulate wholesale or retail trade. The State did not concern itself with investment or employment; it did not even enforce elementary sanitary precautions or prevent the sale of adulterated goods. Co-operators had to arrange everything for themselves without either help or hindrance from the State, which was simply not concerned.

To-day the Co-operative movement finds itself face to face with a very different kind of State, the outcome of universal suffrage and long popular agitation. It can no longer stand aside and manage its own affairs apart from the State, for the State is continually interfering with it. This interference is not peculiar to the Co-operative movement, or specially designed to regulate the movement's affairs; it is simply an incident of the general extension of State activity in the nation's economic life. Moreover, the growth of State services has deeply affected the position of the Co-operative movement, not only in its trading aspects but also as an agency for mutual help. Nowadays the State competes with the Co-operative Society as a candidate for the investment of working-class savings, while on the other side its insurance and assistance services enable the sick and the unemployed to meet many of their problems without withdrawing the savings they have invested in the Co-operative Society.

All this has come about without the necessity, so far, for any substantial changes in the basis of Co-operative organisation. The Co-operative movement has simply carried on, getting more members, selling more goods, and accumulating more capital by methods not much different from those which it adopted in the Victorian Age. Nor have these methods, right up to 1950, served it ill, by the measure of sheer commercial success. The new conditions of living have not rendered them obsolete. The 'Co-op.' is still an excellent savings bank; the housewife finds the 'dividend' as welcome as ever; there is still plenty of room for 'mutual' trading and mutual thrift to work together for good. None the less, competition with the private traders has become keener; the average rate of surplus on turnover and of dividend on purchases has been falling away; and State control has gone some way towards nullifying the Co-op.'s advantage by raising the compulsory conditions of retail trading.

But now at length the Co-operative movement must begin to face a challenge to its traditional assumptions. For it can no longer take for granted that the capitalist environment in which it has been working hitherto will continue indefinitely, either in retail or wholesale trade or in the branches of production in which it is engaged. Since 1945 the further development of the 'Welfare State'—itself at a vast distance from the *laissez-faire* State of the nineteenth century—has gone on to the accompaniment of the opening phases of yet another kind of State—the Socialist. So far, socialisation has barely touched the fringes of the Co-operative world; but it is not likely to stop short at the point reached after only one period of office by a Socialist Government. There is much more to come, though no one yet knows how much, or how soon, or in what order of priority, or even precisely what. This indeterminacy of the next steps gives Co-operators their opportunity to influence the course of events —provided they know what they want and are prepared to work with, rather than against, the Socialist grain. What they cannot have is influence without policy, though that, it seems, is what all too many of their leaders would like best. In order to play their part in shaping the policy of the Labour Party, through which alone they can hope to exert political influence (for the other parties are on the private traders' side), they must have a clear and considered policy of their own; and this policy must be based, not on remaining aloof from the State, but on working closely with it.

This must be so because the basic policies of the new epoch

require overall economic planning as a means to the maintenance of full employment and the furtherance of 'fair shares' for all. The Co-operative movement cannot, even if it would, contract out of the social programme and claim the right to go its own way unaffected by it. It cannot claim that, if the case is made out for a unified system of agricultural marketing, Co-operative farms and marketing agencies shall be exempt. It cannot argue that if, say, the public interest calls for the reorganisation of flour-milling, the Co-operative flour-mills shall be allowed to go on just as if nothing were being done. But it can, and should, claim that the Government, in deciding precisely what to do in such matters, shall take Co-operative opinion into account, provided that Co-operators have constructive, and not merely negative, opinions to express.

It is because they show so few signs of having any constructive proposals to put forward that I have ventured to write this book. Its concrete suggestions may be misguided in many respects, but it is surely somebody's business to get the discussion started. It is also somebody's business to consider, in more general terms, how far the philosophy which the Co-operators hammered out for themselves in the epoch of *laissez-faire* needs re-shaping to fit the epoch of advancing socialisation. I venture to suggest that it needs a good deal of re-shaping, and that many of the traditional ideas and phrases have already lost most of their meaning.

Take for example the word 'voluntarism'. I have suggested earlier in this book that it is really nonsense to talk in the same breath about the voluntary nature of Co-operation and about the coming 'Co-operative Commonwealth' in which all consumers' services will be organised under Co-operative control. What, in this Commonwealth, is to happen to anyone who lacks the volition to be a Co-operator? Is he to go without everything that is supplied only by a Co-operative Society? Or is he to pocket his dislikes, and become a Co-operator because he must—unless he is prepared to starve on principle? The voluntary basis of Co-operation has been of great value in building up the movement, and I have no wish to discard it to-day. But it means a good deal less than it did once, even now; and it will mean less still if Co-operation continues to advance. I want to preserve voluntarism as the basis of the movement, but I do not see how that can be done and capitalist trading be abolished as well, except by giving the individual consumer a choice, between Co-operative Societies and the kind of semi-Co-operative 'Mutuals' I have suggested, as well as by leaving in existence a fringe of small private shopkeeping.

Moreover, Co-operators should beware of clinging too fondly to this word 'voluntarism', which comes to them from a past which, in its passion for *laissez-faire*, was content to go without compulsory education, compulsory drainage, compulsory safety precautions in mines and factories, and a great many other things which it has long been seen to be necessary to provide on a compulsory basis for an advanced, urbanised society. It is not a long step from voluntarism to anti-Socialism, and the best chance of preventing Socialism from degenerating into bureaucracy is to have those who believe in the voluntary spirit acting on the side of, and not against, those who accept the need for compulsion where it is the necessary condition of doing the job properly. There was a time when the distributors of voluntary charity fulminated against those who advocated the development of the public social services, but by now most of the voluntary social agencies have learnt to work in harmony with the statutory bodies. In much the same way, the growth of the State's economic activities makes it appropriate for the Co-operative movement, in the twentieth century, to work in much closer association with the State.

Thus, I do not see why Co-operative Societies need hesitate, when opportunity offers, to act as agents of the State—for example, in supplying *all* the inhabitants of a particular area with milk or coal—even if this involves some departure from the voluntary principle. Nor do I see why Co-operative bodies, in order to extend their range of services, should not be prepared to borrow capital from the State, or, again, to enter into partnership with the State for the conduct of some branch of wholesale trade, such as sugar, or of some branch of production of consumers' goods. Yet again, I see every reason for the Producers'

Societies, which have been always held back by want of adequate capital, to accept State aid in establishing new factories in which to try out, under more favourable conditions than in the past, the virtues of their form of workers' democracy.

For, to come back in conclusion to a point which I made at the beginning of this book, the Co-operative movement can claim a high and honourable place in the structure of the new society only if it is prepared to play an active and imaginative part in bringing that society into being. If, in the barren determination to cling on to what it already has, it allows itself to take up an attitude of sheer obstruction to desirable social changes and to serve as a buffer for capitalism instead of helping the Socialists to supersede it, the great claims made by Co-operators for their movement will go by the board, and the State will be driven to take into its hands enterprises which it had better leave to be organised co-operatively—provided Co-operators are prepared to take the task in hand. It is difficult not to be impatient at the sight of a movement of so vast potentialities quite unable either to make up its mind what it really wants or to think in terms big enough to match its opportunities.

Index

*

For Product Safety Concerns and Information please contact our EU representative GPSR@taylorandfrancis.com
Taylor & Francis Verlag GmbH, Kaufingerstraße 24, 80331 München, Germany

www.ingramcontent.com/pod-product-compliance
Ingram Content Group UK Ltd.
Pitfield, Milton Keynes, MK11 3LW, UK
UKHW022156190926
475702UK00003B/63
* 9 7 8 1 1 3 8 3 3 6 3 8 4 *